D0416706

HOW
BRITAIN
KEPT
CALM
AND
CARRIED
ON

HOW BRITAIN KEPT CALM AND CARRIED ON

Real-life stories from the Home Front

ANTON RIPPON

MICHAEL O'MARA BOOKS LIMITED

First published in Great Britain in 2014 by
Michael O'Mara Books Limited
9 Lion Yard
Tremadoc Road
London SW4 7NQ

A CIP catalogue record for this book is available from the British Library.

Papers used by Michael O'Mara Books Limited are natural, recyclable products
made from wood grown in sustainable forests. The manufacturing processes
conform to the environmental regulations of the country of origin.

ISBN: 978-1-78243-190-9 in hardback print format
ISBN: 978-1-78243-236-4 in ebook format

1 2 3 4 5 6 7 8 9 10

Designed and typeset by Design 23
Illustrations by Greg Stevenson and Claire Cater

Printed and bound by CPI Group (UK) Ltd, Croydon, CR0 4YY

www.mombooks.com

ACKNOWLEDGEMENTS

The biggest 'thank you' I have to extend to those who helped put this book together obviously goes to those people from all over Britain who responded to my appeal and took the time to write down their memories and stories – some long, some short and pithy, all of them painting the broad picture – and send them to me. They form the main part of this book and without them the task would have been impossible. The overwhelming majority were happy to put their names to their stories. In a tiny number of instances, mostly for professional reasons, contributors asked to remain anonymous and I have respected their wishes rather than not use their stories. Similarly, a few were happy for their name to be included but not their location.

Thanks are also due to my daughter, Nicola Rippon, who spent many hours reading hundreds of handwritten letters and putting them on to a computer so that I might more easily work with them.

Last, but not least, thanks to my literary agent, Jo Hayes of the Bell Lomax Moreton Agency, who saw the potential in the idea, to Michael O'Mara Books who were ready to publish it, and to my editor there, Gabriella Nemeth. We all kept calm and carried on.

INTRODUCTION

I f it hadn't been for Adolf Hitler, I would be a Yorkshireman instead of a Derbeian. The decision by the Austrian with the comedy moustache to wage a massive bombing campaign against British cities would prove to be one of the most fateful of the Second World War. It would also change my life for ever, even before it had begun.

At the start of the Second World War, in September 1939, my parents lived in Kingston upon Hull where they had been for four years, ever since my printer father had taken a job on the local evening newspaper. But, in May 1941, they moved back to my mother's hometown of Derby. The reason: Hull was busy acquiring a reputation as Britain's most severely bombed city after London. The Humberside city spent over 1,000 hours under air-raid alert.

So when I was born, in December 1944, it was in Derby, a town still a target, given that the Merlin engines that powered Spitfires and Lancasters were built there, but for some reason one that escaped the very worst of the Blitz.

A few hundred yards from where I struggled into that angry world, outside the offices of the Derby Gas, Light and Coke Company, six escaped German prisoners of war were being recaptured by two policemen and a Corporation bus driver. The Germans had escaped from a POW camp in Staffordshire, but their luck ran out when their stolen car broke down opposite Derby's main police station. After a short chase through the town centre, they were rounded up, the last one collared by the bus driver on his way to start the early shift.

As the bedraggled and thoroughly miserable Germans began their melancholy journey back to prison camp, my mother, unaware that the Wehrmacht had been just down the road, laboured away in our front bedroom with the assistance of the family physician, Dr Latham Brown. My father sat downstairs fiddling with the wireless set, switching between the Bob Hope programme on the General Forces station and Paul Adam and his Mayfair Music on the Midland Home Service. Eventually, getting on for midnight, I appeared, just in time for Christmas.

Five months later I attended the local VE Day street party. Of course, the significance of grown-ups performing the conga along our street, while singing 'Roll Out The Barrel' passed me by. But it is nice to be able to say: 'I was there.'

From her home in the Lincolnshire fenland town of Spalding, my Grandma Rippon marked my first birthday with a postcard showing a cartoon of a small boy and his dog, and a quote from Winston Churchill announcing to Parliament, six months earlier, the German surrender: 'Let us not forget the toils and efforts that lie ahead.' It isn't the sort of sentiment you would normally send anyone on their birthday, let alone a one-year-old. But, then again, life in post-war Britain was going to be tough. Why wrap it up? Or maybe she was displaying a little bit of leftover wartime irony. Actually, I rather doubt that, as you will see.

So I don't remember the Second World War. But as I grew up in the 1940s and early 1950s, 'the war' always seemed to be the main topic of conversation in our family. Even when we went on our annual visit to Grandma Rippon, 'the war' was always on the agenda, especially the tale about the night the Germans thought that they were bombing nearby Peterborough but instead destroyed Spalding Liberal Club. It stood a couple of hundred yards from the Rippons, who, thinking that the Luftwaffe would never bother with an insignificant market town, hadn't thought to erect an air-raid shelter. They soon wished they had. When the sirens sounded and it became obvious that this was the real thing, they all tried to cram themselves under the grand piano that took up half their small dining room. There was much shoving and pushing until everyone was safely installed. All except Gran herself, that is. She was a big woman, a Victorian, and the stern matriarch of the family. She refused to indulge in such an indignity and, instead, sat in her usual chair, defying Hitler to do his worst. In the post-war years, the grand piano still sat hogging that dining room, and the tale was retold many times, Gran still overseeing it all, supreme in the same chair that had survived the bombs.

My parents weren't there to see this comedic episode. They spent the years 1939 to 1941 mostly in the air-raid shelter that they had wisely arranged, with occasional tentative explorations to see what further damage the Luftwaffe had wreaked on Hull. As the centre of that city was steadily being demolished by Goering's air force, each morning my father picked his way through the previous night's rubble to get to work wearing a *Hull Daily Mail* armband so that the police would let him through cordoned-off streets. I still have a faded newspaper cutting showing him and his fellow compositors at the newspaper. Actually, I only have his word for it. The purpose of the story was to show them all carrying on with their work while wearing gas masks. So it seems the most pointless group photograph ever kept as a memento ('That's me, second from the left, honest.'). But there was a war on . . .

Each teatime he would return with the news: 'The docks copped it again last night,' or 'There aren't any houses left in Grindell Street.' Parts of Jameson Street, where the *Mail* offices were situated, were badly damaged. Often my father went straight down to work after a hair-raising night spent fire-watching on the roof of the *Mail* building. He never did find out what happened to his pork-pie supper that disappeared when a bomb exploded uncomfortably close by. The episode became another of those stories.

Their house backed on to allotments and, long before the nightly warning siren wailed out, my parents knew that another raid was imminent because of the frantic activity around the anti-aircraft gun that was sited just over their garden fence. One night, tired of huddling in the shelter, they remained in the house. At the height of the raid, my mother got bored and stuck her head out of the back door to see what was going on. Suddenly there was a high-pitched 'whooshing' noise and my father grabbed her by the hair and pulled her back in. I still have the large chunks of shrapnel that missed her by a few inches.

Things got worse. A young girl was blown into their garden after a bomb fell nearby; the girl survived but her parents, neighbours of my mother and father, were killed. Down the street, three Scottish soldiers died when a blast bomb fell, stripping them naked but leaving their bodies unmarked. Out doing the shopping one morning after a raid, my mother and a neighbour were stopped by an Air Raid Precaution (ARP) warden who told them that a human ear had just been found in the road.

More than 1,200 citizens of Hull were killed and ninety-five per cent of the city's houses damaged in some way or other. When the houses directly opposite my parents' house were flattened, with the blast throwing my mother from one end of their hallway to the other, it was the final straw; they decided it was time to return to Derby. And so I missed out on being a Yorkshireman, and it was all Hitler's fault.

It all sounded rather hair-raising. But what appeared to be a constant theme in all the stories my parents told me was the humour that came through. There was generally a round of laughter when they remembered a neighbour on an outside lavatory, caught with his trousers around his ankles when a bomb fell nearby. There was the woman down the street who wouldn't go to the shelter until she had found her false teeth. 'For Christ's sake,' shouted her son, 'they're dropping bombs, not bloody ham sandwiches!'

They even found amusing the story of the family who emerged from their shelter after one heavy air raid, opened their back door to return to their house, and discovered that the only thing still standing was that outside back wall.

'They had to laugh,' said my mother. I rather doubted it. Indeed, I often wondered if it was just my parents who saw the humour – sometimes black – in all this, or whether it had been a common experience for people faced with war. So in 1978, through Britain's national and regional newspapers, I made an appeal for amusing war stories to be included in a book. The response was immediate. From all over the country, people wrote in with their tales. It turned out that my parents weren't the only ones with a fund of war stories of the humorous kind.

Interestingly, the overwhelming majority were stories from the Home Front, either of the Blitz or of regular service life. It was obvious that soldiers, sailors and airmen serving abroad were enjoying – that should probably be enduring – a wholly different war from those posted at home. Thus, the stories in this book are much more about what life was like in wartime Britain than what it was like in overseas theatres of war.

But, home or abroad, remember this was only thirty-three years after the end of the war, so the memories were still quite fresh. Some respondents were in their sixties and seventies, and had already reached adulthood when war was declared. Their wartime memories were of work or military service. Others were perhaps only in their forties when they wrote to me and so recalled the war through the eyes of a child. If one made a similar appeal today, it would be impossible to gather a similar archive of memories simply because so many of those who responded in 1978 must have since died. I kept collecting material for some time afterwards, always with the intention of producing this book. Various career commitments prevented me from doing so until now.

What prompted me to revisit them was that 'Keep Calm and Carry On' slogan that seems to be everywhere these days and which, when I first saw it, I assumed to be from a wartime poster. It was indeed one of three produced by the Ministry of Information in 1939 when it was intended to raise public morale – or at least prevent it from sinking altogether – in the face of mass air attacks on British cities, and possible invasion. The first two in the 'set' – 'Your Courage, Your Cheerfulness, Your Resolution will Bring Us Victory' and 'Freedom is in Peril' – were soon displayed across Britain.

Yet despite the fact that some two and a half million copies of 'Keep Calm and Carry On' were printed, they never saw the public light of day. In fact, until 2012 when someone turned up to BBC television's *Antiques Roadshow* carrying fifteen of them, it was thought that only two copies existed outside official archives.

Why weren't the posters ever displayed publicly? Well, the intention had been to release Keep Calm and Carry On in the event of an invasion, and that threat had receded. Also, heavy bombing and gas attacks had been expected within hours of war being declared. But it was almost a year before the Blitz started, and gas was never used. Civil servants had misjudged the public's reaction to the war and all its dangers, and the poster would have patronized people who had already shown great courage in the face of the first aerial bombardments. Britons were getting on with their lives. They didn't need a poster to tell them to Keep Calm and Carry On. They were doing that anyway.

So, at last, here are the stories of those who kept calm and carried on without the poster. The stories remain largely unedited because I want the voices to ring out. My intention was that what little tidying there was to be done should not destroy the freshness of these accounts. They were not written at the time, but they were recalled when such memories were still vivid in the minds of those who had experienced them.

Life was difficult, and not just for people on the front line, whether in the army abroad or facing death from the skies over Britain. Even getting to work and keeping the family safe could be a stressful experience. The problems of balancing a home life around wartime work were never more well illustrated than when MPs discussing manpower problems were told by the Joint Parliamentary Secretary to the Minister of Labour that a man sought permission to start work at 8 a.m., rather than 7 a.m., because he had to take his baby to its grandmother's. His wife had to get up at 5.30 a.m. to be at work for 6 a.m., and Gran didn't come off nightshift until 7 a.m. You needed a sense of humour to cope with that.

Of course, it was not just the proverbial men and women in the street that found laughter was often the best way to deal with those dark times. In December 1940, even official British sources could not resist a little humour when they dropped propaganda leaflets along the Dutch, Belgian and French coasts. The leaflets were in the form of a travel warrant and invited German troops to make a one-way trip to England where they would find 'a most cordial reception, with music, fireworks, free swims, steam baths, and many other entirely novel forms of entertainment are provided. Visitors will find their welcome so overwhelming that few are expected ever to return home.' The leaflets were: 'Valid for next summer!'

Humour was indeed everything. When the London home and offices of the actor, playwright, songwriter and wartime intelligence officer Noël Coward were destroyed in the spring of 1941, he took himself off to Snowdonia and, in just five days, wrote the play 'Blithe Spirit'. It premiered in Manchester in June that year, and in London's West End the following month. To get into the theatre, first-nighters walked across boards from a recently destroyed air-raid shelter. If it seems odd that such a frivolous play could have emerged during such a terrible time, let us remember that its author was the man who also wrote 'Don't Let's Be Beastly To The Germans'. Winston Churchill enjoyed the song, but the BBC banned it.

Together, all this confirms what we always suspected: that the British have a rare talent for caustic satire, a gallows humour frequently used to draw the sting or fear out of a threatening situation, and, above all, stoicism in the face of even the greatest adversity. It was all put to particularly good use during the Second World War as Britons strove to rebuild their homes, factories, shops and, most of all, their lives. Almost everyone seems to have kept calm and carried on.

GLOSSARY OF ABBREVIATIONS
USED IN THIS BOOK

AA – Anti-Aircraft

AC2 – Aircraftsman 2nd Class

AFS – Auxiliary Fire Service

ARP – Air Raid Precautions

ATS – Auxiliary Territorial Service

CD – Civil Defence

CO – Commanding Officer

ENSA – Entertainments National Service Association

GCO – General Commanding Officer

HE – High Explosive (bomb)

JP – Justice of the Peace

KP – Kitchen Patrol

LDV – Local Defence Volunteers

MEF – Middle East Forces

MO – Medical Officer

MP – Military Policeman

NAAFI – Navy, Army and Air Force Institutes

NCO – Non-Commissioned Officer

NFS – National Fire Service

RAF – Royal Air Force

RAMC – Royal Army Medical Corps

RASC – Royal Army Service Corps

REME – Royal Electrical and Mechanical Engineers

RNVR – Royal Naval Volunteer Reserve

RSM – Regimental Sergeant Major

SAS – Special Air Service

USAAF – United States of America Air Force

UXB – Unexploded Bomb

VAD – Voluntary Aid Detachment

WAAF – Women's Auxiliary Air Force

WRNS – Women's Royal Naval Service

WVC – Women's Voluntary Corps

WVS – Women's Voluntary Service

YMCA – Young Men's Christian Association

PUT THAT
LIGHT OUT!

Heinz Guderian invented the Blitz. Sort of . . . The German army general advocated a tactic based on speed and surprise, where light tank units and fast-moving infantry were supported by air power. Hitting hard, moving swiftly, creating havoc, it was the blitzkrieg or 'lightning war' that Adolf Hitler adopted to overrun Poland in 1939 and enslave Western Europe the following year. It was blitzkrieg tactics that drove the British Expeditionary Force back to Dunkirk in 1940, and their most awesome use was at Operation Barbarossa – the German attack on Russia in 1941.

To the British, however, the Blitz came to mean only one thing: nightly aerial bombardment by the Luftwaffe. Throughout the autumn, winter and spring of 1940–41, the nation came to dread the wail of air-raid warning sirens, particularly in the big cities of London, Birmingham, Sheffield, Coventry, Hull, Manchester, Bristol, Liverpool, Glasgow and Belfast, but also in smaller towns and even, on occasions, isolated villages.

Altogether some 43,000 civilians died during the Blitz on Britain. Almost 140,000 more were injured, and more than a million homes were damaged or destroyed. Yet far from dampening the spirits of

British men, women and children, this danger and deprivation served only to strengthen their resolve. And it was laughter that seemed to be the national anaesthetic. It helped the British through the bombing, not least because they could chuckle at themselves, which was just as well when one considers what outsiders sometimes thought of them.

According to Walter Graebner, London correspondent of the American news magazine *Time*, the besieged Londoner was a very special creature:

> *Londoners are admirably suited to standing up to the blitzkrieg. Small and wiry, they can step quickly into low, cramped Anderson shelters and dugouts. Phlegmatic, they express practically no emotion when death and disaster strikes near.*
>
> *Unused to a high standard of life, they don't grumble when they lose their home or possessions and their jobs. So long as they can have three or four cups of tea a day and go for walks, their two most cherished desires have been satisfied.*
>
> *Because for centuries they have braved one of the worst climates in the world, sturdy Londoners do not find leaking roofs and damp shelters unbearable. Because they have fought so many wars in the past, they don't look upon this war as a calamity, even though it's coming down on top of them.*

So Londoners just had to laugh at themselves. As one newspaper commented of Graebner's description, it conjured up an astonishing picture of a race of inscrutable dwarfs, crouching philosophically under a steady stream of water pouring from a busted ceiling, surrounded by dripping walls and moving only for an occasional walk in the world's worst climate.

The paper ended: 'Mr Graebner's Londoner seems a cross between a happy alligator in a damp cave and an undersized tramp asleep in a tea-chest.'

That they were certainly not – but when it came to raising a laugh with a quip, there wasn't a breed to beat them. When an old man filed into an air-raid shelter one night, carrying under one arm a long-handled spade with which to deal with incendiary bombs, and under the other a harp – presumably for a little entertainment – one cockney said to her friend: 'Blimey, there's a bloke wot's backed 'imself both ways.'

As far as Britain was concerned, life had to go on as normally as possible. Nowhere was this more apparent than at golf clubs where special rules had to be devised to deal with the interruption caused by air raids.

In 1940, Richmond Golf Club in Surrey conceded: 'In all competitions, during gunfire, or when bombs are falling, players may take cover without penalty for ceasing play.'

However, another rule said: 'A player whose stroke is affected by simultaneous explosion of bomb or shell, or by machine-gun fire, may play the ball from the same place. Penalty: 1 stroke.'

A typical example of golfers' sangfroid was shown by the following rules: 'The position of known delayed-action bombs are marked by red flags at a reasonable – but not guaranteed – safe distance.' And: 'A ball moved by enemy action may be placed as near as possible where it lay, or if lost or destroyed, a ball may be dropped not nearer the hole, without penalty.' Well, you couldn't say fairer than that.

Indeed, British sport in general took the Second World War in its stride. In July 1944, at Lord's, a cricket match between the army and the Royal Air Force was stopped when a doodlebug was heard approaching the ground. The players lay on the turf, and spectators disappeared under the stands. But the rocket flew over the ground and landed in Regent's Park. Middlesex and England opening batsman Jack Robertson dusted himself down and celebrated the narrow escape by hitting the next ball for six. An outraged *Wisden*, the cricketer's 'Bible', later reported that this was 'the first flying-bomb to menace Lord's during the progress of a match'.

Watching football as the Battle of Britain raged overhead could be a tiresome diversion. The Home Office had ruled that play must be stopped whenever the air-raid alert sounded. Clubs attempted to counter this with a system of 'spotters'; even after the alert sounded, play would continue until the spotter on the roof of the stadium signalled the actual presence of enemy aircraft.

It wasn't just the bombs that caused problems, though. The blackout was as much a nuisance to sportsmen as it was to the general public. But they coped with it. Southampton FC's coach driver, returning from a game at Cardiff, became lost in the blackout, then he hit a brick wall, and finally the vehicle suffered a burst tyre. The players were forced to spend the night in the coach, not arriving back in Southampton until lunchtime the following day. The players of Wycombe Wanderers had probably the worst experience. After a Great Western Combination game at Slough, the Wycombe team had to walk the fifteen miles back to High Wycombe.

The blackout also caused problems for players training after work. Harold Atkinson of Tranmere Rovers recalled the dangers: 'The part-time training was on a Tuesday and a Thursday and you ran around the ground at your own risk. We used to sprint down the side of the pitch in the dark, and there were more injuries caused by training in the blackout than there were in proper matches.'

Young and old, people coped. Writing to America in thanks for Bundles for Britain – a collection of clothing and other items sent from the USA for those bombed out of their homes in Britain – an elderly Scottish woman said: 'When the air-raid siren goes, I take down the Holy Bible and read the twenty-third Psalm, then I put up a wee prayer, take a wee dram of whisky, get into bed and pull up the cover. Then I tell that Hitler to go to hell.'

Going the rounds in Hull – as we have already seen, the second most bombed city in England, with ninety-five per cent of its buildings damaged or destroyed – was this definition of the perfect air-raid warden:

> *He must be as brave as a lion, strong as a bullock, wise as an owl, industrious as a bee.*
>
> *A warden must be prepared to be blown up, thrown up, burned alive, shattered, splattered, flattened, and be able to act as wet nurse, dry nurse, doctor, undertaker, Spitfire Fund collector. He must be agile, servile, deaf, dumb, and unconscious if necessary. Above all he must be able to speak BBC English, repair a phone, anticipate the sirens, and suffer criticism without thought of retaliation.*

The war often brought out the best in people, especially during the Blitz. One North-East farmer, anxious not to abuse the system for claiming compensation for damage, registered his claim thus: 'Repairing broken glass in piggery £3; replanting hedge £1; bomb crater fifteen feet deep by thirty feet across is well placed for making a new farm pond that will be entirely acceptable to animals.'

The Blitz certainly produced some wonderful characters.

In December 1944, Chaplain K. Evans, RNVR, who had worked as a curate in London during the earlier war years, told the *West Australian* newspaper about the time he asked an elderly member of his Bermondsey congregation how she managed to remain so calm at what was the height of the Blitz. She told him: 'I comes in, I sits down and reads me book. I says me prayers. I says: "To 'ell with 'itler," and then I goes to sleep.' Like that Scottish lady, that was her recipe for a restful night.

Relating another anecdote, Evans said that when a stick of bombs was dropped it was often possible to count them and estimate where the later ones would land. This happened once when he was conducting a service. The congregation counted. The sixth bomb fell on one side of the church, the seventh landing on the other side in the road. But in relating the story to a friend afterwards, one old lady said: 'And when we got outside there was the creator right in the middle of the road!' On occasions, incendiary bombs were referred to as 'insanitary' bombs.

On another occasion during a raid, the curate went with an ambulance to a public house that had received severe damage. Right in front, and in the middle of the road, a woman was sitting laughing uproariously, an empty glass in her hand. The blast had sucked her out of the door, and when the curate asked her why she was laughing, she replied: 'Blimey, that's the first time I've been out of the pub before closing time.'

Bombed-out shops and stores managed to carry on, with notices such as 'More Open than Usual' advertising that they were still trading, although when beer was in short supply, one publican's chalked notice told would-be customers simply: 'Sold Out. Gone Out.' Another sign, spotted on a bombed-out store, read: 'This is nothing! You ought to see what the RAF have done to our Berlin branch!'

And when passers-by saw an office manager and his secretary seated on the pavement outside what was left of their office, with a typewriter, cups of tea and a plate of biscuits on their shared desk, they knew that they were keeping calm and carrying on.

In August 1940, Pulitzer Prize-winning American journalist Ray Sprigle was in England to report on the war and to see just how Britain was keeping calm and carrying on. That August, filing a story from 'the South-West Front', Sprigle told of an experience he underwent when the air-raid siren sounded as he slept in his hotel.

Sprigle stumbled down to the air-raid shelter, to find that he was the first to arrive. It was, wrote Sprigle, a 'de-luxe' shelter with white-topped tables set out in an adjoining room that also contained a piano.

One by one, the other guests came in, quite calmly, and sat around while the manager's wife poured them tea as the raid went on overhead.

Eventually one guest, uninvited, began to play the piano, with one finger, knocking out probably the only tune he knew.

'Wouldn't it be grand if Jerry dropped a bomb on him?' said another guest. That did not daunt the player, but then one lad in the corner decided to compete by doing impressions of a cat and dog fight, and a hen laying an egg. Then everyone started singing, first 'South of the Border' and then 'The Last Roundup'.

The hotel manager told Sprigle that he recently visited a friend. He arrived to find the friend picking through the wreckage of the family home. When the previous air raid had started, the man had put his wife, two daughters and the family's two pet dogs under the stairs, while he and his small son sheltered in the sitting room. A bomb had come straight down the chimney.

The man said that he had shaken his arms and legs and 'as none fell off, I figured I was all right', and then he extracted his wife, daughters and dogs from under the stairs that had collapsed on top of them. Remarkably, none of the family was injured. As they emerged into the street, an old man was walking past. He stopped to survey the wreckage of a pub on the corner that had also suffered a direct hit.

'Hell of a thing,' said the passer-by, 'when an Englishman can't get his dram or his beer because of that blighter in Berlin.'

'All over England,' wrote Sprigle, 'people are taking these air raids in their stride . . .'

I was working in London, in Cannon Street, at the time of the doodlebugs – the flying bombs that came over, then cut out, and fell to earth. It was nerve-wracking. Once that engine stopped, you just waited for the explosion.

One lunchtime, people were streaming out of their offices when we heard one coming over, so we just dived onto the pavement – which was muddy as it had been pouring with rain – and then there was silence, followed by this almighty bang a couple of streets away. We all got up and started off again when over came another. Same thing – dive on the pavement, silence, big explosion.

As I was getting up yet again, a little chap in front of me, wearing a cap, was also climbing to his feet. He looked at me and said: 'Gettin' kinda 'umdrum, ain't it?'

Etta Stern, Surbiton

One night we were in a communal shelter in Bermondsey, just after the warning siren had sounded, when a friendly ARP warden shone his torch down the stairs and shouted: 'Any expectant mothers down there?'

Quick as a flash, a rich cockney voice shouted back: 'Cor blimey, mate! Give us a chance. We've only been down 'ere five minutes!'

Honor Helm, Hastings

In the early days of the London Blitz we were living in Stratford, E15. Prior to going to the Anderson shelter it was our practice to cut sandwiches and make flasks of tea because we knew that Jerry would regularly arrive shortly before 6 p.m. This particular night the East End was his target and it was very hectic. He was giving us a good going over.

My wife and I, with our baby son, were quite comfortable inside the shelter, and around about 1 a.m. we decided to have a cup of tea. After about half an hour, I had a feeling that I would have to run the gauntlet to the outside loo, but owing to the shrapnel from the anti-aircraft guns I decided to wait until a lull occurred.

But eventually it became a question – excuse my French – of shit or bust.

Suddenly, miraculously, a lull occurred and I said: 'Now's my chance!' I dashed from the shelter and reached the toilet safely enough. I proceeded to drop my trousers, but just as my bottom touched the toilet seat, a mobile 3.5 ack-ack gun went off about fifty yards from the house. My head hit the toilet ceiling and I simply ran and dived headlong back into the shelter, causing quite a commotion because I landed on the tea table and on my wife. My trousers were still around my ankles and to this day I don't know whether I accomplished what I'd set out to do.

J. Edmonds, London

> I was in Bobby's restaurant in Bournemouth and the sirens sounded. One of the waitresses, a lugubrious type, seized an umbrella, put it up and said loudly: 'Peace in our time.'
>
> G. RODDA, PUTNEY, LONDON

I'm hard of hearing, so the sirens and the bombs didn't unduly worry me, as very often I didn't hear them. One night, there was a particularly bad raid over London and many buildings were destroyed, some not far from my home. In the morning my neighbour came in for coffee and exclaimed: 'What do you think of last night's terrible raid?'

'Oh,' I replied, 'I slept all night, didn't hear a thing.'

'Well,' she said, in such a jealous way, 'you're just lucky that you're deaf!'

Cecilia Morgan, Golders Green, London

It was during the Blitz on London in 1940 and a stick of bombs had fallen in Pembridge Crescent, Notting Hill Gate, and failed to go off – UXBs we called them.

It was thought that one had penetrated the sewer (a brick one about thirty feet deep) and the bomb disposal sergeant said that he would remove it. I asked him how he would get it out and he said he would go into the sewer, tie a rope to the bomb and pull it out. So I gave him a safety lamp to use, and then he said, 'Oh, by the way, are there any rats down there?'

And when I said, 'Yes,' he said, 'Well, I'm not going down there, then. We'll dig for it instead.' And he made his men dig a hole thirty feet deep and got the bomb like that. He was prepared to face an unexploded bomb – but not a rat!

G. A. Shapland, Lancing, Surrey

Bodiam in Sussex, 3 September 1939. Lots of Londoners were picking hops. We'd just heard that we were at war. About half an hour later, we heard a lot of planes coming. As we'd already been kitted out with gas masks, we just put them on, thinking they were planes with gas. And there we sat, in the hop garden, with our masks on. Eventually some Londoners told us: 'It's all right, mate – they're ours!'

L. Beaney, Tenterden, Kent

As a young woman during the Second World War, I lived with my crippled mother and an aged aunt in a ground-floor flat in a large block, surrounded by similar blocks of flats and a few houses.

During an air raid, we would sit at the end of an inner corridor to be safe from splintered glass, as windows always blew inwards with a blast. On one occasion there was a direct hit on the block next door, and its flying masonry descended on our own block, causing it to shiver and shake for what seemed like an eternity. Finally it decided to stand firm. Terrified, we clung to each other in the dark on the floor where the blast had hurled us. The flats had coal fires and separate anthracite boilers, and the smell of soot was stifling. All doors but one were off their hinges and, judging by the noise, every window was out.

Suddenly a flickering light appeared where our front door had once stood; a dark figure, holding aloft a lighted candle in one hand, made its way unsteadily towards us. It was the lady from next door, simply covered with soot, her red-rimmed blue eyes shining out of her black face. In her other hand she held an almost spotless pair of white corsets.

'Isn't it disgusting?' she said. 'New today and now they've got a bit of soot on them!' She was very shocked and had no idea that she looked like a black minstrel. Very soon her equally sooty husband, who bore a bottle of Chartreuse and a mug, joined her. And we all shared a loving cup by candlelight.

Suddenly two more excited figures entered the corridor. One was the lovely daughter of our neighbours, barefooted, dark hair streaming over her white nightdress; the other was her fiancé. The house nearby where they lodged had been razed to the ground and they were the sole survivors. You can imagine the emotional impact on the girl's parents. There was also a young schoolmaster we knew. There seemed to be safety in numbers.

By the time I had brewed some tea during a lull in the bombing, the ARP arrived to ask how many refugees I had and if I could cope. I could, and bedded everyone down in the corridor with blankets and pillows.

Just as we were dozing off, there were loud screams from the lavatory on the corridor and the sound of fists pounding on the door. The poor girl in the nightdress had gone in there and the door, being the only one left on its hinges, was out of true. The lock had jammed and refused to yield to pressure. Eventually the ARP had to return with a pickaxe to free her – not an easy task without injuring her.

Twenty-two years later, I met this girl again in Brighton. She'd grown into a poised and elegant young matron and invited me to her charming home where we laughed about the caricature element in that horrific night of long ago.

Mrs C. Tennant, London

Although I worked as an electrical and magnetic instrument maker, in the evenings I played in a band. At the height of the Blitz, we were playing at a function in Altrincham, in a large hall that doubled up as the local ARP headquarters.

On this particular evening, there was a big raid and many of the dancers left, either to go on ARP duty or just to get home to their loved ones.

Suddenly there was a huge explosion, the building rocked around the clock, and the doors on all the emergency exits were blown open. I was ready to run off stage when I saw the pianist still tinkling away, so I stayed too, even though there was now nobody dancing.

Eventually the all-clear sounded and we had time to take stock. The first thing I noticed was a large switchboard for the lighting and telephone. Someone had pinned a notice to it: 'If the alarm bell goes once, raiders approaching; if the alarm bell goes twice, raiders in the vicinity; if the alarm bell goes three times – the bloody building has been hit.'

Anyway, by now the pianist had joined me. I said: 'That was a brave thing to do, carrying on like that.'

'Carrying on?' he said. 'I couldn't stand up for fright.'

Frank Budgeon, Manchester

We'd just had a bad raid and in the morning the street was littered with rubble and broken glass. A group of workmen arrived to clear up the mess. Suddenly one of them grabbed a sweeping brush, danced a little jig, and shouted out: ''itler's blinkin' 'ousemaid, that's all I am.' It made us all laugh and, for a moment, forget what had happened to us.

H. R. Harvey, Southampton

We lived in a three-storey house in Keyham, close to HM Dockyard. One night there was a particularly bad raid and all of us except my elderly grandmother – she was in her eighties – were huddled under the staircase. Grandma sat defiantly in her chair against the passageway in a sort of alcove.

We all sat there, listening to the awful sound of the heavy bombs, breaking glass, and incendiaries coming down like falling rain. Grandma seemed oblivious to all this, but kept complaining: 'There's an awful draught round my back and legs.'

Getting no answer, she shouted to her long-suffering son: 'Sid! Go and see if the front door's closed.'

Uncle Sid emerged from under the stairs and went dutifully along the passageway. He was gone an awfully long time and Grandma kept saying: 'Where's he got to?'

Eventually, he reappeared. She said: 'Well, was it open?'

Uncle Sid said: 'Yes, it was open all right. And if I could have found it, I'd have closed the bloody thing for you.'

Actually, although our house hadn't suffered a direct hit, when the raid was over we found that it was so badly damaged it was uninhabitable.

Iris Brokenshire, Liskeard

I remember a story from the *Lincolnshire Standard* at the time: A Post Office engineer was ordered one night to go to an anti-aircraft battery site because their telephone was reported out of order. It was raining and a severe blackout was in force. In addition, the sentries on that particular site had a reputation for being trigger-happy. The engineer tried to announce his approach by calling loudly at intervals: 'Telephones! Telephones!' Suddenly, almost at his elbow, a voice said: 'Trying to sell 'em, mate?'

R. M. Gale, Littlehampton

My mother was having tea with an old friend when the sirens sounded. Bombs started dropping close by and my mother and her friend, who was a very corpulent lady, both dived simultaneously under the dining table. My mother's stout friend couldn't get her entire frame beneath the table and was left with her posterior jutting out.

My mother laughed and said: 'That's a fine target for Hitler!'

Anonymous

I was in Forest Gate Maternity Home in 1940. I had to stay there nearly three months, as I'd been very ill through kidney trouble while I was expecting my first baby. I had an uncanny knack of hearing the bombs coming down before anyone else, so I used to tell everybody to duck under the bedclothes. Well, I eventually had my baby boy on 9 October at 11.30 a.m. About an hour and a half later, at dinner time, there was a raid with no warning sirens. The nurse was just going to get my baby for me to feed him, when I heard a bomb falling and shouted at everyone to duck. I did so myself and, thank God I did, for when it was all over I emerged from under my bedclothes and I couldn't believe it. My bed was covered in glass. Even the window frame was on the bed. I stuck my head through it and said: 'I think I've been framed!'

Mrs W. M. Shaw, Ilford

My mother and father were huddled in the shelter during a raid one night. The old lady next door had joined them and she was complaining about the cold. So my father said that he'd brave the bombers and go and make some cocoa. About fifteen minutes later he returned with this big jug of lovely steaming-hot cocoa. The old lady was salivating at the prospect of it, so much so that her false teeth fell out and the bottom set went straight into the jug.

Everyone just looked at each other. Then my father fished them out with a spoon. It's safe to say that the old lady had the jug to herself. And every time she shared the shelter after that, they kept a close eye on her dentures.

Ted Harrison, Derby

In 1943 I was in my late teens. Because of the damp in the Anderson shelter, my father, mother and I decided to stay indoors. My parents slept under the dining-room table, me in a recess away from the French windows, on feather overlays, plus top covers. At that time, Jerry, if he still had bombs left after a raid, dropped them anywhere. Well, one dropped nearby and the soot came down the chimney and covered me. My father got the vacuum cleaner out to clean it off me, still holding his long johns with one hand and cleaning me with the other. He was six feet tall. It was the funniest sight I'd ever seen! He didn't think it at all funny, though.

Jesse Aitkens, Broadstairs

I was about ten years old and living in Grimsby when we suffered a particularly bad air raid. Our family – Mum, Dad, myself and two small sisters – made our way to our garden shelter. Our neighbours were doing the same. We settled ourselves down and realized we were in for a bad night with planes overhead, bombs dropping and anti-aircraft guns going off. Suddenly my dad said: 'Heads down and pray like mad!' Then, we all heard it getting closer and closer – a loud whistling sound. A bomb dropping!

I remember thinking that I didn't want to die, but Dad said: 'That bomb's taking a helluva long time dropping!' and shot off down the garden along with several other terrified and confused neighbours. Well, we waited and waited. When he returned a few minutes later he said, angrily: 'That blasted Mrs So and So!' It seemed she'd put on the kettle to make a cup of tea and the whistling sound had been her kettle! She never dared to use her kettle during night raids again.

Joan Campbell, Grimsby

We had several bombs drop where I lived. One night we were in our air-raid shelter when my brother came in the doorway. Just then, one of the bombs seemed to drop very close to us. My brother, very keyed up, said: 'That's blown my bloody hair all over the place!' The funny thing was – he was bald!

MRS E. A. HOOSON, SWINTON, MANCHESTER

My story takes place on 6 September 1940, when I was living in Liverpool. It was the day before I was to be married and I was thirty-eight years old. The air-raid alert sounded at 8 p.m. My brother, my youngest sister – who was in bad health with TB – and myself all got under the stairs. My mother insisted on going to bed. Her philosophy was that, if your name was on a bomb, you'd get it anyway, and she wasn't prepared to lose sleep over it. Well, sorry to say, that night we got a direct hit on the front of the house. Luckily, it was only a 250-pound bomb. But my dear mother was trapped in bed with the roof on top of her. We screamed for help from the ARP wardens and, finally, they got her out alive. She was very shocked and had a bad cut on her forehead. Well, the funny part of it was when the ARP warden said to her: 'I can still hear your chimney clock chiming!' she replied: 'I only paid thirty shillings for it off a Jewish jeweller. He must have been an honest man!' With the neighbours' help we cleaned her up and, after a cup of tea, things didn't seem so bad. Sadly, I lost four sisters and two little nieces in the Christmas Blitz that followed.

Phyllis Essex, Malvern

After every air raid – and they came every day – all the services had been badly damaged. This particular day there was just one small pipe left, with a little water dribbling through it. People came with buckets, bowls and saucepans to get water. Us nurses invented a guessing game as to whether it would be a bucket, a bowl or a saucepan. It helped to get us through the day.

L. Davis, Tipton, Staffordshire

Like many hundreds of others past military age, I joined the Auxilliary Fire Service just before the outbreak of war. I did my training at the Bethel Street fire station in Norwich and at a brewery around the corner. Eventually Norwich acquired a fire float. One Sunday morning, after I joined the crew of about eight men, we did a practice run to Colman's Mustard Works and, after a good drill, the officer in charge, who was my brother-in-law, gave the order to go ashore for a break and a smoke. The ground was a bit marshy were we were to step off the float and, grabbing my rubber boots with one hand, I slipped on mud and fell into the river, much to the amusement of my comrades and the workers at Colman's.

On another occasion at Colman's, following enemy action, we arrived as the front wall of the building collapsed straight down, sinking the barges that were full of grain. Colman's had its own small works fire brigade and they worked alongside us. After a very hard shift, I arrived home to discover that, not only was I covered in spots of black soot from the engine, but that I had my rubber boots on the wrong feet.

D. Bushell, Norwich

In April 1941, the Luftwaffe again picked on Norwich as their target for bombing with high explosives and incendiary bombs. Huge fires were started at Carrow Works, which was the home of Colman's Mustard. I was then a section leader in the Auxiliary Fire Service, stationed at Lawrence Scott's Gothic Works. We were called to attack the fire at Colman's from across the river. After about three hours – around two o'clock in the morning – we wanted to get in closer to the fire. This meant crossing the river and taking the hose over. To do this, a boat was needed. Looking along the riverbank, I saw, reflected in the water, a rowing boat. It was just what we wanted. I said I would get in, so the crew could hand the required equipment to me. The riverbank at that spot was about five feet down to the water. So I jumped down. But, instead of landing in the boat, I went straight through the bottom into six feet of water and oily mud. I didn't know until then that the boat had no bottom. With just my head out of the water, it took four men to pull me out on the end of the rope. They had to put me nearer to the fire to dry out before I could carry on.

A. G. C. *Tompkins, Norwich*

One Friday night during the Blitz on Norwich, there was a fire at a timber yard just opposite our boat station. The crew were fully engaged using two forward water nozzles and two after nozzles, plus some hand hoses, when a market trader, known as 'Alf the Handbag King' from Bethnal Green – he came to Norwich every Friday and stayed near our station ready for business on Saturday – offered his services as he couldn't understand why two burly firemen were required to manage only one hose. Of course, he didn't realize the strength required to hold a hose steady. He was duly kitted out and instructed how to stand his ground. Full pressure wasn't put though at once, but when it was, he was down on his back and drenched with water. We never saw him again.

D. *Bushell, Norwich*

It was a very stormy evening. The rain was really lashing down when the sirens went. My boyfriend and I rushed to the air-raid shelter, which was under a church. Women and children were wailing, screaming and crying – when we reached the steps leading down, there was a little Jewish air-raid warden with his torch showing the way down. His tin helmet settled on his ears and, with his long mac, he cut quite a comical figure. As people passed by, he kept repeating, over and over, in a heavy Eastern European accent and something of a lisp: 'Thix theps down and mind you don't trip!' As each of us walked down those six steps, we repeated his little 'catchphrase' and within five minutes everyone, frightened children included, were laughing and joking. He was only a little man 'doing his bit' but he cheered us up no end.

Mrs C. G. Atkins, Bourne, Buckinghamshire

I was living temporarily in Streatham Hill, SW2, and was helping the local voluntary services. During one air raid, a block of flats close to Streatham Hill Station received a heavy blast. I was helping an ambulance man assist a lady who was pregnant. Five small children surrounded her. All were, thankfully, unhurt, but since the windows etc. were gone, and all utilities like gas and electricity were affected, we were taking them to temporary shelter. It was 1 a.m., so they were all in their nightclothes. The mother was a very cheerful cockney type. I was endeavouring to fit a small boy of about six years old into some trousers, handed to me by his slightly older sister. The boy was shrieking and not cooperating. 'I don't want to put my trousers on!' Amid all the chaos, and with the AFS and the ARP all around, his heavily pregnant mother looked at her five children and said: 'You see! He's just like his dad. My husband has always got his trousers off!' I thought that it was commendable that a woman with so many little ones to take care of, not to mention another on the way, could still joke about her predicament.

Mrs A. Olins, Finchley

I was in London throughout the Blitz. My mother and I would sit by the fire reading until about half past ten and then we went to bed. We had no air-raid shelter. The house rocked sometimes as many bombs dropped very near – but we'd no wish to be out in the cold garden. In 1944, when the VIs were coming over, I was getting into bed when one just cleared our house and burst about sixty yards away. All the windows came in on top of me, but by a miracle, I wasn't badly cut.

Earlier in the war, during the Battle of Britain, near us there was a big field in a built-up area, although it had never been used for anything. I was told that it was a burial place for hundreds of plague victims. One Sunday morning we had a daylight raid and I saw, for the only time, German aircrew bail out. I knew some bombs had fallen nearby and when the all-clear sounded, I went out and walked to this field and a bomb had dropped on it. An elderly woman came along with an armful of bones. I said: 'Whatever have you got there?' And she said: 'Bones – we're supposed to keep them for salvage, aren't we?'

Stanley Norman, Brighton

Although I was born and raised in South Yorkshire, I spent the Second World War in Eastbourne where I was partly responsible for checking damaged property. At one of the few houses still occupied in a supposedly evacuated, leafy street, there lived three very typical 'Old Lace and Frilly Ladies'. The area, which was close to the town hall, had been repeatedly bombed, but it never seemed to worry these three. One afternoon I was making a hurried check after a daylight raid, and I knew some nearby houses should really have been knocked down. As I got to the doorway of the house occupied by the three ladies, I found them busily brushing up plaster, dust and garden soil that had blown into the front hallway. They were not happy and told me that had they not had to keep the front door open – which was the practice to avoid worse damage from the force of any blasts – then the mess with the garden soil would have been avoided.

On the outer fringes of Eastbourne there was an electricity station. Opposite stood a row of council houses that were, for the most part, uninhabited. Following raids it was usually my job to check those that were still lived in. At one house, belonging to a real 'Cor Blimey' type whose husband was serving in the army, I got no reply although the house appeared to be intact. Just to be sure, I went around the back to the garden, where I found her pointing at a hole and a heap of wood and broken glass. When she saw me she shouted out, as if it was my fault: 'Look what that so-and-so Hitler has done to my old man's greenhouse!'

L. G. Lee, Croydon

I had a small guesthouse in Clacton, about one hundred yards from the seafront. There were two NAAFI girls staying with me, as they worked in the Towers Hotel that was their headquarters. Naturally, most of the properties were taken over by the military, which organized dances etc. at their mess. One of the girls had been invited to one of the army dos and on that particular evening enemy action put out the lights in the NAAFI and shook the building considerably. This girl was worried about having a wash on the premises as time was cut fine for her date. The water had been turned off, but she groped her way to the kitchen sink and 'felt' some water in the bowl. She hurriedly washed her face and put some powder on. She was adept at the latter as she often did this in the dark of the cinema. As she'd a greasy skin, she liked her make-up. The air raid didn't last long and the lights were soon back on in the mess. As she entered everyone stared at her. She looked such a sight. She didn't realize that the bowl contained soot that had been blown down the chimney during the raid. Our glamour girl is teased to this day by those who've passed the story on, especially since there were some really dishy officers there that evening.

Ivy Moulton, Clacton

We lived in Ilford at the start of the war. Our neighbours had been offered an Anderson shelter in 1938, but had refused. By September 1940, the London Blitz had begun and they changed their minds. By this time, however, the demand for shelters was high and they had to wait. In the meantime, they dug the hole, ready for the delivery of the shelter and we took some palings out of our fence to enable them to use our shelter. One night there was a particularly heavy raid. We were already in the shelter when Mrs McC came down in her nightdress with a thick eiderdown wrapped around her. When I tell you that Mrs McC was around fourteen stone, you'll know that we weren't surprised when she got wedged in the shelter entrance. Her husband, Jack, began to push her from the rear, as we were pulling her from inside. Suddenly she fell in head first, leaving the eiderdown wedged in the entrance. Fortunately, she wasn't hurt and we all had a good laugh.

After a while, Mrs McC asked where the gas masks were. Jack said he hadn't got them and that they must still be on the kitchen table. Jack was a silly old fool, said Mrs McC, and he'd better fetch them 'before we were all gassed to death'. So Jack went inside to fetch the masks.

After a while we heard a terrific crash, followed by a few muffled choice words, then another crash, followed by Jack falling head first down into the shelter. He'd put on his gas mask in the house and, of course, couldn't see where he was going. He fell down the hole he'd dug for his own shelter, hit his head on the crossbeam of the fence and knocked the snout of the gas mask upwards and sideways so that it finished somewhere above the region of his left ear. He never heard the end of that.

45

We left Ilford soon afterwards and came to Derby. Some years after the war we went back to Ilford for a visit and happened to be walking past the McCs' old house, just as some workmen were removing an Anderson shelter from their garden.

Eileen Godfrey, Derby

I have poor hearing, which is why I wasn't in the army. One afternoon, I was reading my newspaper as I travelled home on the tram when, all of a sudden, I realized that the tram had been stopped for quite a while. I looked up to find no one in sight. No driver, no passengers, no conductor. Then there was a terrific explosion. A V1 had dropped about one hundred yards away. Eventually, out came the driver, the passengers, and the conductor. They'd all been hiding under the seats, having heard it approaching. They thought I was a cool customer, still sitting there reading.

Stanley Norman, Brighton

My friend's husband had extremely bad eyesight and had taken off his spectacles before getting into bed. He placed them on his bedside table along with a jam tart that he'd taken up with him in case he got peckish in the night. He was fast asleep when the sirens sounded. As a fire warden he had to be on duty, but preferred to ignore the summons. His wife nudged him with some urgency to 'go and do your job'. The room was in total darkness and after scrambling out of bed, he groped for his specs, floundered around the room in the dark and eventually ended up in the wardrobe. When the light went on he was wearing his wife's sunglasses and clutching a sticky jam tart.

The same couple were again woken up by the sirens. Firebombs were falling all over place and, again, the wife urged her husband to do his duty. This time he went to the window, saw the mountain of blazing fires and asked: 'Which one would you like me to tackle first?'

When I was directed to go on fire duty for the first time I would also have preferred to ignore the summons, but my mother reminded me: 'You've got to go out and help the girl next door. You're both on duty.'

Sticking my helmet on my head I went outside, assuming that the other girl, who knew the ropes better than I, would guide me along. She wasn't there. In fact, there was no sign of life in the whole street. There was I, facing pockets of fire and puzzling as to what I could do alone. Suddenly, as I stood there pondering on this problem, a piece of shrapnel hit my helmet with an ominous ping. That was enough. Crouching under the porch I rang the bell of our flat and my mother came hurrying downstairs. 'What's wrong?' she asked. 'I've been hit,' I told her. 'And I'm not going out there again. That girl hasn't shown up and I'm not fighting the war alone.'

My mum wasn't at all impressed and it wasn't until next morning that I could find the piece of shrapnel as evidence of my 'injury'.

'That?' said my mother sarcastically, 'That's nothing . . .'

Peggy Saunders, Richmond

It seems that our next-door neighbour was a bit of a coward. Every time the sirens sounded, he used to panic and run like mad to the air-raid shelter. We lived at Hucknall, only a few minutes from the Rolls-Royce Works aerodrome, so the sirens went fairly frequently. One day it seemed worse than ever. First the warning sirens, then the all-clear sounded, one after the other all day long. Each time our neighbour did his 'minute-mile'.

In the evening my mother was on her own with her four children because Dad was on the evening shift at Rolls-Royce. By a quarter to midnight, she was fed-up of going back and forth to the shelter. She was in bed, just going off to sleep, when the siren went off again. Through the wall she heard a mad scramble going off in the bedroom of next door, and our neighbour running downstairs, taking them about four at a time. She heard him shouting in the back garden to his wife to hurry up. When his wife joined him, my mother heard him ask where we were. His wife replied that we were still in bed. At this point he began shouting up to my mother's window urging her to get up and get to safety. My mother opened the window and peered out. She told him she was staying where it was warm and dry and comfortable and, if she was going to die, that was where she was going to do it. Our neighbour wasn't impressed. He called her 'mad' and went off on his 'minute-mile' once more. My mother laughed as he nearly tripped himself up trying to put on his trousers and getting two feet into the same leg hole.

Once, while I was playing for a sergeants' mess dance at a POW camp near Rochdale, there was a breakout of prisoners. The first we knew was much later when a sergeant said to me: 'It was all your fault! You shouldn't have played "The Prisoner's Song" followed by "If I Had the Wings of a Swallow".'

Hannah Wheatley, Belper, Derbyshire

One late spring night in 1940, the first air-raid warning sounded in Smethwick. At the time I was newly married. My husband was in the armed forces and I was living in rooms with a very old and very deaf lady. I was in bed and, since it was a very warm night, I was wearing no nightdress. However, at the sound of the siren, I jumped out of bed and ran to the old lady's bedroom shouting: 'Mrs B, the air raids have started! The sirens are going!'

She, poor soul, being very deaf, said, 'What?'

I said, 'The bulls are blowing!' The 'bulls' were the pre-war factory sirens telling everyone it was time to go to work.

With that, panic-stricken and, I am afraid, cowardly, I ran downstairs, grabbed a coat and a pair of sandals and raced to the nearest shelter, which was down a steep hill in the local park. On my flight I tripped and cut my knee. Reaching the shelter, which was dark and empty, I stood there trembling for what seemed like hours but could have been no more than five minutes, when a man and two small children entered. I spoke. He nearly jumped out of his skin; he thought I was a ghost. I told him that I'd fallen, and with the aid of a match – in the circumstances I was glad he'd no torch – he bound my knee with a clean handkerchief. A few minutes later, more terrified people came in and my 'Sir Galahad' said he would take me to the first-aid post when the all-clear sounded. There the first-aid officer dressed my knee and I managed to hold my coat together this time.

When he took me home, we found that poor Mrs B had barricaded herself in her room. When she peeked out of the window and caught sight of the first-aider still wearing his helmet, she panicked. 'The Germans have got her! Please don't have me, I'm only an old woman!'

The first-aider was an old neighbour and knew Mrs B well, and realized there was no point in him trying to calm her, so ran down the street to fetch her son. After some difficulty, Mrs B's son managed to get to his mother, who clearly still thought she was in the hands of the Germans, and was yelling and crying. Only when she saw her daughter-in-law did she calm down. I didn't stay much longer with Mrs B, but I reckon I was the first air-raid casualty in Smethwick.

Mrs E. R. Smith, West Bromwich

We were in London during the Blitz, and we had an Irish lodger living as one of the family. Her name was Sheila McSweeney and she was about twenty-six. She never worried about bombs dropping.

All she ever did was read a book and smoke a fag, and nothing took her away from these. Well, one night in 1941 we were getting a terrific bombing. All the docks were ablaze and our street was hit very badly. In the space of one night, a high explosive and an oil bomb were dropped on the street. Then another bomb fell but remained unexploded, and then a Molotov Breadbasket [a bomb that combined a high-explosive charge with a cluster of incendiary bombs that were released as it fell] and several incendiaries were dropped. My parents and sisters were all in the shelter in the garden, while Sheila stayed in the kitchen with her book and her fag, never bothering about the carnage in the street. My brother and I were racing in and out of the house, fighting the fires as they broke out, but every time we came indoors, she was still sitting and reading. We kept asking her to come and give us a hand, but never once did she look up or answer us. We were absolutely beat at the finish, so for the last time of asking we begged her to help. Well, she put down the book, took the cigarette out of her mouth and retorted: 'This is not my war, it's your war. So you can get on with it!' With that she put the cigarette back in her mouth and carried on reading, leaving my brother and I not knowing whether to laugh or cry. What an answer. As if the Germans would know there was an Irish neutral in the house and not attack it. Anyway, a short time later she was in the thick of it, and if anyone deserved the George Medal that night, it was Sheila McSweeney.

Eric Cutmore, Bourn, Cambridgeshire

During the war I had three apple trees in my garden, which I painted with whitewash to keep insects away. One moonlit night, when we expected an air raid, my next-door neighbour looked out of her bedroom window at the back of the house, saw my trees and panicked. She ran down the stairs to her family shouting: 'My God! German paratroops, dressed in white, have landed in Mr Barnett's garden!'

A. A. BARNETT, COLINDALE, LONDON

Between 1940 and 1943, I was employed as a senior nursery attendant in Oxford, with a group of forty children aged between three and five. The nursery had originally been a large home but Lord Nuffield had taken over the building as part of his factory. The nursery unit was housed in an old youth hostel with a beautiful garden.

We had several air-raid alerts, thankfully all false, but the children found a wonderful game imitating the siren, after which an older child would take a smaller one, usually carrying it to a large oak tree.

One day we were visited by an air-raid warden because the children's imitation of the siren was so good, it had been fooling the neighbours!

Josie Nicholson, Ivybridge, Devon

During the summer of 1940, my husband had gone down to the local pub for an evening drink. Around 9.30 p.m. and alone at home, I decided to step outside for some fresh air. Our cottage stood on a bank and from the garden I saw what I thought were German paratroopers dropping from the sky. Quickly, I ran the 300 yards towards the pub to start the alarm. Everyone, including the landlord, put down their pints and rushed outside, climbing up the steep hill to our cottage. The first man up there, however, seemed less alarmed.

'You fool! They're barrage balloons!'

Mrs A. Taylor, Shifnal, Shropshire

In June 1944, I was travelling to my job as an invoice typist with the LNER at King's Cross Goods Way in London. It was a beautiful day and I was wearing a white dress and shoes and carrying a white bag. My train was sitting in Vauxhall station and the carriages were packed when suddenly one man shouted at me: 'Get down, missus!' A flying bomb's engine had cut out over the station. Everyone else threw themselves to the floor, but I took one look and saw it was filthy. There was no way I was going to lie down there. So I just huddled up and prayed.

Gladys Lutterloch, Yeovil

During the war one of my friends, Dorothy Griffiths, decided to have a party and, as she lived in a flat, her aunt and uncle gave permission for her to hold the party at their Salford home, a small terraced house with no bathroom and an outside lavatory. As the party drew to a close, a few of the boys were too late to get back to their various camps and lodgings in Eccles and so were invited to stay overnight. All was quiet until the return of the aunt and uncle. The uncle had a sudden thought about what might happen if any of the lads had to answer a call of nature during the night. So he grabbed a spare chamber pot, went upstairs, knocked on the bedroom door and shouted: 'Jerry's here!'

There was utter chaos as the men scrambled down the stairs, pushing the uncle to one side. They thought there was an air raid and were heading straight for camp!

Mrs Frances Sheridan, Bolton

One of the Group 2 staff, London Civil Defence, was a very tidy secretary known as Rosie. We were on night duty, but resting as we did when no alert was on. Then the air-raid siren sounded and we rushed down to the basement room to man our posts. Poor Rosie was quite unaware at having run down there dressed only in blouse and petticoat!

Leila Mackinlay, London

The scene is my grandmother's air-raid shelter. It must be about 2 a.m. The shelter is full of people, maybe about a dozen or so. It is easy to hear people in adjacent shelters in gardens on either side. Laughter, singing and so on. Suddenly everything goes quiet. A pair of very booted heavy feet begin to walk down the long path towards the shelter. Thud, thud, thud. Is it an enemy parachutist who has landed nearby? Everyone is holding their breath. Left, right, left, right, clump, clump, clump. And then, in a very loud voice: 'Achtung!' Utter terror on everyone's faces. Until they realize it was my uncle playing a trick. I don't think they knew whether to kick him or kiss him.

Brenda Shaw, Kingston upon Hull

Aunt Maggie had been evacuated to the country. When Uncle John came home on leave, she moaned and moaned about having to live in a converted stable.

'Oh well,' said Uncle John, 'our Lord was born in a stable.'

'Aye,' replied Aunt Maggie, 'but he wisnae paying seven shillings and four pence a week.'

Sheila McGerhan, Glasgow

The nearest air-raid shelter was a communal one at the end of the road. One night we were all running madly down the street while the guns boomed overhead and flares dropped around us. Halfway down the road, one of us noticed that Nanny was missing. She was standing in the street, gazing admiringly at the flares and wanting to know who had put them there.

Mrs B. M. Hipperson

One morning, in the early hours, just Mother and me at home. It's a warm summer's night and the windows are open. There's suddenly the sound of heavy breathing in the bedroom. My mother gets out of bed, warily, to search for our 'intruder'. After creeping into the other rooms and finding no such man, yet the heavy breathing getting louder and louder, we discover it is the noise of the breeze whipping through the ropes attached to the barrage balloon in the neighbouring playing field.

Brenda Shaw, Kingston upon Hull

There were some strange sights after the air raids on Hull. There was a house where the front wall had been blown off but you could see almost every piece of furniture still in its place, like a doll's house with the front just taken off. After one raid, a complete fish-fryer from a fish and chip shop that had been hit was sitting on the roof of a house on the other side of the street. But people just got on with it, and it was the little things that bothered them. One old lady who lived opposite my friend was being lifted out of the rubble of her house and she kept asking for her false teeth. Apparently, they'd been in a glass of water beside her bed. The Civil Defence men told her not to worry about her dentures, they could be replaced. But she said that she wasn't leaving without them: 'I'm not letting people see me without my teeth.'

Phyllis Rippon, Derby

Flat 66 in Newport Buildings, Covent Garden, wasn't a luxury apartment. But in May 1941 it was a comfortable enough home for seventy-two-year-old Rose Heffer – even after the Luftwaffe had dropped a bomb nearby and caused sufficient damage for the building to be declared unsafe. So Mrs Heffer ignored cracked walls, loose brickwork and the absence of doors and windows, and continued to live there.

She ignored, too, the notice pinned to an outside wall, declaring the building unsafe and forbidding anyone to enter it. When a night-patrol policeman heard someone moving around, he investigated and found Mrs Heffer alone, sitting by a roaring coal fire. Yes, she'd read the notice but she didn't have anywhere else to go, so she was stopping where she was.

The policeman couldn't agree and instead took her to the police station. One week later, she appeared at Bow Street Magistrates' Court accused of failing to obey a police order not to enter a building.

She told the court: 'I wasn't in there long. I went in to wash after I'd buried my poor son who was killed in that terrible raid. Anyway, the flat isn't in such a bad state. I wish you could see it. They're going to repair it this week.'

Hearing that she was now sleeping down the Tube and spending the days wherever she could, the magistrate, Mr Fry, told her: 'Well, I hope that someone takes care of you.' Then he dismissed the case, leaving Mrs Heffer to keep calm and carry on, just like she was trying to do.

Anonymous

One night, at my other grandmother's house, as twelve of us gathered, the air-raid warning sounded. There was no time to run to the shelter before an uncle shouted: 'Duck! There's a bomb coming!' I flew under my mother's skirt, two aunties scrambled under the table, and the rest cleared the room in seconds. Only when we heard nothing but silence did we realize it was another false alarm.

Brenda Shaw, Kingston upon Hull

During the war I lived on a hillside above Hebden Bridge in Yorkshire. Up on the moors there was a searchlight squadron and I remember very late one night my mother and I were alone – my father was on fire-watching duty – when there was a knock at the door. Outside stood two soldiers, who were obviously very drunk. One of them had a black cat in his arms, which he tried to sell to us for ten bob. We told him we weren't in need of a new cat, since the one in his arms was ours.

J. Purdis, Essex

Football matches in London were the worst. They were always being interrupted. I used to take my ukulele with me and when we came off, we'd have a sing-song in the dressing room until the all-clear sounded and we could resume the game. George Formby numbers were particularly popular.

Jack Wheeler, Birmingham goalkeeper

My mate's father was an ARP warden. On his first night the sirens sounded and he was struggling to put on his kit. He finally managed to get everything on – uniform, gas mask, cape, steel helmet – except his new rubber boots – they were like wellingtons – that he'd left till last. He planted his feet in them and took one step forward, only to fall flat on his face. They were still tied together with string. He was rolling around on the floor, his wife was shouting to him that the Luftwaffe was coming, and he just looked at her and said: 'Well, they'll have to wait because I'm not ready yet.'

George Bradshaw, London

I was a gunner on a gun site on a bomber station in 1940 when bomber stations were being heavily attacked by German aircraft, and a football match had been arranged between the RAF personnel and the gunners who were operating the low-level-attack guns. There was this match, being played near my gun site. For that reason I was allowed to referee the game. In the middle of the game, we hear a low droning sound. It was a day of low clouds. We look up at the aircraft and it is a Ju88, a German light bomber. And so I raced to my gun, whipped on my steel helmet and respirator that we had to wear – you never knew when there was going to be a gas attack – and manned the guns in refereeing kit. We had to abandon the game.

Ken Aston, international football referee

At Friargate Station, Derby, ticking was heard coming from a parcel. With war imminent, and recent IRA bombings, this was no time to take a chance. The suspicious package was placed in a bucket of water and firemen called. It was relief all round when the 'bomb' was revealed to be no more than a small ornamental clock belonging to a passenger on her way to Staffordshire. Laughter all round . . .

Bernard Buckler, Derby

I remember one game between Charlton Athletic and Millwall at The Valley in 1940. There were only sixty seconds remaining when the air-raid warning siren sounded. The raid was a heavy one with shrapnel from nearby anti-aircraft guns falling on the stadium. The 1,500 spectators took cover and when the all-clear sounded, the game resumed and the final minute played out. Millwall won 4–2. Can you imagine, people just hanging around while an air raid was taking place, just so that they could see the final minute of a football match where the result was already beyond doubt? I think that shows just how much people took things in their stride.

Frank Broome, Ottery St Mary

During the Blitz one bomb scored a direct hit on a house a few doors away from ours in the East End. It was a right mess, and out of it a big bedstead was thrown right across the street and landed on its legs. And, would you believe it, there was a pair of trousers, neatly folded, still hanging over the rail.

But I think the funniest thing I ever saw was in the West End. It would have been late in 1944, and I was in a long queue, waiting for a bus. Suddenly we heard a doodlebug. Then all went quiet and everyone chucked themselves on the floor. We had no idea where it was going to land. Fortunately, for us at least, it was some streets away. Everyone got back up and the queue reformed. Then I felt a tap on my shoulder. I turned around to see a 'city gent'.

He said: 'Excuse me, but I think I was in front of you.'

I won't tell you what I said to him.

George Foster, London

FOR KING AND COUNTRY

It was something that my mother often used against my father. Even thirty years after VE Day, she would, when provoked, remind him of the day in September 1939 that he asked her to stand in a queue and find out how he could avoid military service. To be fair, her version of the event was tailored to suit her point. On the day war broke out, my father was a Linotype operator – a typesetter – employed by the *Hull Daily Mail*. As such, he was in a 'reserved occupation' and, like most other skilled tradesmen, would have found it difficult to be accepted into the armed forces even if he had wanted to join up. Which he clearly did not, but all he had asked her to do was to pop down to the Labour Exchange and collect the relevant forms.

He was not alone. In 1939, and unlike in 1914, there was no patriotic surge to join the Colours. Memories of 'the last unpleasantness' were still raw. Conscription had ended in 1920, but in May 1939 the rapidly deteriorating international situation saw the introduction of the Military Training Act. Single men aged between twenty and twenty-two were liable to be called up as 'militiamen' to mark them as separate from the regular army.

They were even issued with a civilian suit as well as a uniform, just to underline their status as part-time soldiers who would undergo six months' basic training before being discharged into a reserve, from where they would be recalled for short training periods and an annual camp.

But before the first intake had completed their initial six months, war was declared and they found themselves regular soldiers. The National Service (Armed Forces) Act had been passed and now all men between the ages of eighteen and forty-one (by 1942 the upper limit had been raised to fifty-one) were liable for military service, except if they were medically unfit, of course; or unless they were in one of those coveted reserved occupations like lighthouse keepers or newspaper Linotype operators.

Many servicemen on the Home Front found themselves billeted with civilians. My parents took in men from the Royal Signals who were stationed at a nearby telephone exchange. One of them stood six feet eight inches tall, and was universally known as 'Nelson', after the column, I suppose. Another, a Russian, was some kind of electronics genius. He was also an accomplished musician who spent his off-duty hours playing classical music on the family piano, to the delight of my parents and his army colleagues alike. Until, that is, he made a dramatic exit. One hot summer's afternoon, two military policemen hammered on the front door, looking for the Russian. Seconds later, he leapt out of the open front-room window and fled down the street, the Redcaps in pursuit. My parents never saw him again and never learned of his fate, although my mother soon discovered that, as he made his escape, the mysterious Russian had grabbed a row of pearls given to her by her cousin Fred who, before the war, had been a rubber planter in Malaya. He was now languishing in the notorious Changi prison after being captured by the Japanese while serving in the territorial Johore Volunteer Engineers.

'Oh well,' she said later, 'I suppose the poor man was desperate.' She hadn't a clue as to what the Russian had done to attract the attention of the authorities, and she didn't really care. She always had a soft spot for a rebel and the Russian's role in bringing a little colour into an otherwise drab and difficult world was more than sufficient compensation. For years after the war we had his business card, printed in the Cyrillic alphabet. Sadly, through several house moves, I lost it long before becoming interested enough in his story to research it further. I still do have, however, a pre-war Russian banknote that he left behind. Perhaps it was some kind of payment for the pearls after all.

From all accounts, the soldiers were welcome guests but, a few weeks after I was born, Nelson and his fellow signallers took leave of our house. Nelson kept in touch, returning to visit a few times after the war. I have the faintest recollection of this giant in khaki, so I assume he must have remained in the services. Before he left us, however, Nelson had one more duty to perform. A couple of weeks into January 1945, I was baptized at St Werburgh's Church in Derby, a few yards from where the German POWs had been recaptured three weeks earlier. Nelson was there, acting as a proxy godfather for Uncle Jack, my father's brother and a Desert Rat who had fought in the Royal Artillery with the Eighth Army at El Alamein. Uncle Jack was by now serving in Palestine; for some reason, the army wouldn't let him come back just to be my godfather.

The best he managed was a Christmas card from Bethlehem, which was nice.

Even animals served, and in 1943, the People's Dispensary for Sick Animals created the Allied Forces Mascot Club in order to recognize animals and birds that were serving the Allies during the war. A cat called Andrew became the club's mascot. Andrew did not himself go to war, but as he was stationed in London he had to endure air raids on the capital, although it was reported that he kept calm and carried on sleeping through most of them. But he also seemed to know when a V1 rocket attack was due and when Andrew took cover, everyone else knew that it was time to do so. Weighing more than six kilos, he was a fawn-and-brown tabby with a spotless white front, tummy and 'socks'. But, best of all, he boasted an inverted 'V for victory' on his nose. Winston Churchill no doubt approved.

I was a photographer in the forces and my assistant and I had been working in an army vehicle depot. The officer in charge was telling us how a vehicle that would not start had them all baffled until somebody noticed that a small bit of dried mud had sealed the reserve fuel tank, covering the small hole in the fuel cap, thereby stopping the air from entering and allowing the fuel to be drawn through to the engine. Well, the following day we were assigned to an army scheme that was in progress on Bodmin Moor and, making our way across the moor in a very remote area, we came across an American army ambulance that was broken down. So we pulled up and asked what was wrong, and the driver and his mate said that when they switched over to the reserve fuel tank the engine showed no life at all.

I tipped my assistant the wink and he strolled round the vehicle to check for mud on the fuel cap. We were in luck . . .

My mate quietly knocked the mud from the cap and we both walked to the front of the ambulance. We told the driver and his mate that we had not long returned from filming in Africa and that, while there, we had picked up some witchcraft that might help him. We told them to stand by the ambulance and rest one hand on the bonnet while raising the other hand in the air. They were to repeat after us the special magic words that we would recite. We went down on one knee and began to recite a load of mumbo-jumbo that we made up as we went along. After a while, we stood up and confidently told them that the engine should now start. On the second push of the starter, low and behold, the engine sprang to life. You should have seen those Yanks' faces! They gave us chocolate and some other gifts and drove off full of praise for African witchcraft. We found out later that the two British cameramen who had learned witchcraft from Africa were the talk of the American unit.

Chas Keith, Malton, North Yorkshire

It was just after Dunkirk, at an airfield near the Norfolk coast. Everyone was jittery. I was a lance bombardier on an anti-aircraft gun. My mate was a bombardier. All units were at a stand-to. Everyone, including the locals, was wondering, 'Where will they land?'

Early one evening, my pal and I went for a walk and a pint. Having discussed what everyone assumed was the imminent invasion, we arrived at a small local pub and decided to start it on our own. Outside the pub rested a bike and inside, one country worker talking to the old landlord.

'The invasion has started,' said my friend. 'Give us two pints.'

'Get these chairs outside,' he ordered, which I did.

'And get these pictures off the walls!'

'What for?' said the landlord.

'The maps go there,' I said. 'This is now Division HQ.'

All of this was carried out at great speed – including drinking our beer. I'd stacked the chairs and pictures against the wall.

'They should be arriving shortly! Let's take a look.'

Gazing professionally down the road, I said: 'What next, bombardier?'

'Every man for himself,' he said, jumped on the bike and was gone.

I took to my heels and ran after him . . .

L. R. Dyke, Great Yarmouth

It was in late 1940 that I was on a course at Harlesden. We were bedded down in a disused factory and had to provide a guard during the night. More a case of the usual 'bull', actually. I was on one night when, at about 10 p.m., a plane could be heard approaching at quite a low height. He suddenly appeared overhead and commenced to fire a burst of tracer down the High Street. Of course, we were not supplied with any ammo, although only the good Lord knows why. So I rushed into the company office and yelled: 'Quick, sarge, give us some ammo, there's a bloody Jerry out there.'

My thought was, of course, that with the plane at such a low altitude, I might be able to score, at least if only to let the blighter know that someone down there was alive to the danger.

The sarge replied: 'The ammo's in the safe!'

'Well, for Pete's sake, open it then!'

'Can't – the orderly officer's got the key.'

'Well, call him!'

'He's not here. He's gone to the pictures!'

Stan Lynn, Woodford Green

As an army officer undergoing flying training in 1942, prior to taking up duties flying army aircraft, I had reached the stage where it was time to do my first solo cross-country flight. My progress up to that stage had been achieved in shorter time than the rest of my group, so it was not without some cockiness that I climbed into the cockpit, taxied across the airfield and took off on my first flight out of sight of my instructors.

My course was a three-legged one and I completed the first two safely but, during the third leg something affected my judgement and I realized that my navigation had gone wrong. After circling around I made a big mistake, I began to zigzag and after about two hours' flying, with one eye on my fuel gauge, I began to wonder how much longer I could remain airborne.

It was then that I saw, under my port wing, what was obviously an aerodrome – although not my own! Happy again, I headed into wind, made a reasonably good landing, got out and began to saunter across to report my arrival. But it was only as I entered the building that I realized my position – an army type reporting to the RAF that I was lost.

However, they did their best not to show me too plainly that they were amused and I was given a meal and some drinks, while arrangements were made to advise my chief instructor. Only later did I really become embarrassed – when a plane arrived from my Flying Training School, with two pilots, one of whom was to fly me back to base.

Alan Cox, Epsom

The time was June 1940. I had been in the army all of two weeks, but there had been little formal training as our new Regiment 'A' Co, 6th Buffs [Royal East Kent Regiment], was still being formed. So far it had been just a few days to form a platoon, then a week on the rifle range, and now we were at the former *Daily Sketch* holiday camp at Dymchurch in Kent. On the parade ground we were taught the rudiments of standing guard and then, in pairs, our first two hours of night guard. In a field.

The purpose was, I suppose, to watch for parachutists and I know we were keyed up for anything. The night was cloudy and, with the moon, there was a mixture of moonlight and darkness.

Suddenly my mate said: 'Look at those two men at the far end of the field!'

I looked and, sure enough, there were two men bent double and creeping along beside the hedge. We both panicked a bit, I think, and tried to remember what the sergeant major had tried so hard to teach us.

I said: 'What do we do?'

'Challenge them!'

'Who? Me?'

'Yes, you know, "Halt! Who goes there?"'

Somewhat nervously I did just that, but there was no reaction from the men. Now we were for it, I had to challenge again with the knowledge of what followed if they did not respond. They didn't, they just carried on with their slow advance along the hedge.

Now, the sergeant major had stressed that if the enemy failed to respond to a third challenge then we were to open fire!

So, at my third challenge: 'Halt, or I fire!' I released the safety catch, put one up the spout and, with my rifle at my shoulder, prepared to pull the trigger. It was only when I'd actually put pressure on the trigger that the two men at last responded – with a loud 'Moo-oo!'

It was a black and white cow, its front and back ends split by a black patch, thus providing the 'two crouching men'.

The sergeant major never heard of that episode, but he did hear of the sheep that was shot on the golf links, and the man on a cycle brought down by a bayonet through his front wheel when he failed to stop.

R. A. Cook, Grantham

The permanent accommodation at my flying school was limited and many of the trainee pilots were housed in tents pitched in a single line in the shadow of a high hedge.

During what was a really hot summer, one of the trainee pilots, Lieutenant John Hemmings, used to regularly strip off and wash down with water from a canvas bucket outside his tent. One day a voice – an excited female voice – was heard to exclaim from the other side of the hedge: 'There you are, I told you so! He does it every day!'

Alan Cox, Epsom

During a wartime army exercise, dressed as a civilian I captured a complete camp, including the commanding officer, for which I was promptly transferred to a training camp in the north of England.

News of my triumph had gone ahead of me and it had obviously been decided to take me down a peg or two. I arrived to find that I'd been placed on duty all weekend, which was a big joke in the sergeants' mess as they were all going into the nearby town for a big party.

I borrowed a Jeep and found a chemist and squared him with ten bob [50p]. He made up a purgative much like cascara [a plant known for its laxative properties] in powder form. I went into the mess half an hour before guard mounting and dosed three teapots in the spout and awaited results. The powder would work in about two to three hours.

The first sergeant caught was waiting for a bus with his girlfriend. Two more had caught a bus back to the barracks but they were delayed. Another came into the guardroom but the door to the toilets was locked. The RSM was on his way to the wagon lines. He borrowed a bicycle but never made it. All were back in barracks by ten o'clock.

An anonymous army sergeant, Bognor Regis

In March 1941, I arrived at Uxbridge to attend initial training for my RAF police course. We were given a lecture by the accounts officer and asked if we would care to make a contribution to the CO's fund. He explained that there was a box outside his office and he would appreciate it if all donations could be placed in an envelope for his attention. After the lecture I discussed this problem with my new comrades. We decided that, since most of us were married, we couldn't afford to donate anything. About a fortnight later we were all in the classroom awaiting the arrival of our instructor when he burst in waving an envelope. His face was livid.

'Who's the funny man that sent this letter to the accounts officer?'

He took the letter from the envelope and read it out: 'The wages of sin are death, but the wages of an AC2 are a bloody sight worse!'

He never did find out who sent that letter . . .

A. Jones, Huntingdon

Two sergeants were sent on 'initiative training'. Off they went in full kit and were allowed only a half-crown [13p] between them. They had to travel into another county and were told to 'find the master of the Beaufort Hounds and ask him to sign your pay book'.

The two men found the home of the master of the hunt, Badminton House, and rang the doorbell. The butler who answered told them that the duke was away. He was about to close the door when a female voice from within said: 'Don't send them away. Let me speak to them.'

To the amazement of the two young men, they saw that it was Queen Mary, mother of King George VI. After listening to their story, she said: 'As the duke is out, will my signature do?'

She took the two bewildered sergeants into the house and wrote in their pay books: 'Certified that the holder came to Badminton House, Mary R.'

Alan Cox, Epsom

During the war I was in the RAF and attached to an Australian squadron in Scotland. As you know the Aussies have a rather rare sense of humour, so I'll tell you the following incident.

An Aussie airman was washing his dirty overalls in a bucket of petrol in the hanger and a friend of his who was passing said: 'Hello, cobber, are you washing your undies?'

Then quickly came the reply: 'No mate, I'm washing my overies!'

LAC C. H. Campbell

On the Friday we arrived at RAF Uxbridge, we received instructions on the procedures when entering a church on church parade. On climbing the third step before entering the church you were to take off your hat. The following Sunday everything went according to plan until half the squadron were in church and then one poor chap forgot to take off his hat as he reached the third step. He had just taken another step when the booming voice of the parade sergeant bellowed from behind: 'Take your bleeding hat off in God's House!'

A. Jones, Huntingdon

I was in the Durham Light Infantry and later in the KOYLI [King's Own Yorkshire Light Infantry]. During our training at Brancepeth Castle, we were duly sorted out. Those with two persistent left or right feet were put in 'awkward' squads, and of course you will realize that any display of men donning brand-new uniforms looks a sartorial shambles. I recall one lad in our company, a Scot we called 'Little Jimmy Brown' in training, stood out like a sore thumb. He was even a traumatic experience for the training staff. It was March and the weather was damp and cold. Jimmy wore two of almost everything. He said it was a shame he could wear only one pair of boots at a time and one greatcoat. He went to bed like that, the greatcoat aside. Of course, this meant that he was always one of the first ready for breakfast and parade. But, after a few days, it became obvious that he only ever washed his face.

One morning, the PT instructors took a firm hand with Jimmy. He was always late for PT because it took him so long to remove all that extra clothing and change into his gym gear. Eventually one of the instructors and two lads escorted Jimmy into the bathhouse and well and truly laundered him.

None of us was quite sure whether this was just an act to get out of being in the army, or whether it was a quirk of his personality. Either way, he persisted and eventually was discharged for being unfit for active service.

W. D. Donkin, Sunderland

There were some Canadian air-gunners who were awaiting posting to the gunnery school. They were put into the charge of the station warrant officer. He was a really nasty piece of work and did he give these poor Canadians the runaround – all the dirty jobs he could think of went their way. Time came for the Canadians to be posted. In the NAAFI that night they invited the station warrant officer for a farewell drink and presented him with a parcel. He couldn't resist opening it there and then. Inside was a cardboard box and inside that was an assortment of homemade wooden soldiers. On a piece of paper was written: 'You've f***** us around while we've been here, now f*** these around!'

A. Jones, Huntingdon

I was a lance corporal in the Royal Engineers. After lengthy overseas service, I arrived back with my base in Yorkshire. The CO there informed me that, for the next few months, before my discharge, I was to be transferred to another unit. I was then told to report to the station sergeant for further instructions.

'Pay attention and listen carefully!' instructed the NCO as he precisely outlined my journey to Victoria Station, Manchester, and then on to my new unit a few miles away. The sergeant droned on and emphasized how important it was to follow his detailed information.

'Understand everything?' he finally demanded. And, although I was somewhat in a whirl, I managed to meekly agree. As I stood to attention before being dismissed, I was throbbing with emotion and would dearly have loved to embrace my new-found hero – this superb, sublime sergeant.

After all, my new unit was only round the corner from my own home!

Thomas W. Makin, Blackley, Manchester

Before going on my course, I went on three days' leave. My wife examined my uniform and didn't like the way my eagles were sewn on my greatcoat. So she unpicked the stitching and re-sewed them. After my leave I reported to RAF Uxbridge and, the following Friday, was the CO's parade and inspection. Most of the other blokes were picked up for their haircuts but, just as I was congratulating myself, the parade officer's voice bellowed in my earhole: 'Who lowered your eagles?'

I froze on the spot but managed to reply: 'My wife, sir. Are they wrong?'

'They're wrong all right! They're the bloody wrong way round!'

A. Jones, Huntingdon

At Warminster in 1941, there was a Sergeant Thatcher who would keep his squad drilling on the parade ground as he stood in the sergeants' mess having a pint and bawling his orders through the open window.

One day, though, out on Salisbury Plain, we were undergoing driving training in a personnel carrier. When you were driving downhill, you had reverse steering. In other words, when you pulled the right stick you turned left. We had an instructor who chewed tobacco. We were sailing merrily along, downhill, doing a fair speed. The instructor shouted that there was a steep drop ahead and we had to turn quickly. Too late! We shot off into space, then landed with an almighty bump! The instructor swallowed his baccy, went blue in the face and began to choke. We saved him, although he didn't seem too pleased.

Roy Barker, Thornton-Cleveleys

A few months after infantry training at Brancepeth Castle, we joined our Durham Light Infantry battalions and departed for Scotland, where we took part in a large-scale exercise. Sometimes in these types of operations, live ammunition was used and the powers that be had to allow for errors and accidents taking place. Officers acting as umpires, wearing white armbands and dashing all over the place, would come up and say: 'You've been wounded. He's been killed. They've been taken prisoner by the enemy.'

If you were 'wounded' you would have a label tied on you with details of the wounds. If you were a so-called 'morphine case', or had a wound that forbade any drinking, then sometimes you would lie there for days, depending on how long the exercise was supposed to take. The idea was to be as realistic as possible. During the exercise, we had to make a five-mile march followed by an attack. At the end of the attack an umpire told us that our ration truck had been captured and, as the make-believe should be as real as possible, we should wait fourteen hours for our food. When the umpire finally arrived with our rations, we were told that our platoon would soon be reported 'missing or wiped out'. Well, none of us wanted to be 'missing', so we duly walked away in various directions to the nearest town or village. We were supposed to return to camp within a reasonable time of the end of the exercise. Some of the lads certainly made the most of being 'missing', visiting cinemas and so on. A few were taken into motherly homes. A very small number simply disappeared for good.

W. D. Donkin, Sunderland

About halfway through the war, I was on loan to another unit as a driver with a Morris truck and Bofors gun in a town, somewhere in the south-west of England. During the middle of one bitterly cold January night we were in convoy. I had a crew of eight in the back of my truck and by my side was the sergeant in charge. He had replaced an officer who had been taken ill. The exercise was called Spartan, which was a good name as there was about a foot of snow on the ground. Although it was against regulations, we had all removed our boots, but were travelling in silence, as per our orders. We stopped while the other officers checked our location when all of a sudden, the sergeant yelled, looked down at his feet and in his cockney voice cried out: 'Bloody hell, rigor mortis has set in!'

Leslie C. Skinner, Polegate, Sussex

At times there were so many troops staying in Catterick Camp that it was impossible to keep them all employed. I've never drunk so much tea in my life. We spent all day wandering from café to café. At pay parade the men would mill around 'baa-ing' like sheep. They were bored to the back teeth and almost out of control. To get the men out of bed, one corporal would urinate in a bucket and throw it on the fire. The stench . . .

Roy Barker, Thornton-Cleveleys

Pioneer Corps sergeant to a private, presumably in need of a haircut:

'Are you married, Athorne?'

'Yes, sir!'

'Have you any furniture?'

'Yes, sir!'

'Well get rid of those bloody sideboards!'

LESLIE RANDALL, LAMBETH

I served from start to finish of the war. A cockney sergeant had a squad drilling and he had one awkward recruit that he could make nothing of.

The sergeant decided to get some background information and asked about the recruit's family.

'My father was a baron,' said the recruit.

The sergeant replied: 'That's what your mother should have been!'

Mr S. E. Smith, Essex

At Stob's Camp, near Hawick in Scotland, in 1942, we often went out on night manoeuvres. Imagine the clatter as we roared through Hawick. A local copper complained that they made him wear rubber soles, yet allowed us to awaken the dead. The units ran a 'passion wagon' [transport to a local dance] to town from the camp. One night an errant trooper was late for the returning truck. He chased after it down the street. All his mates were leaning over the tailboard laughing at him. With their weight, the tailboard broke and they all fell out. The athletic trooper leapt over them and into the truck. He rode, they walked, so he had the last laugh.

Roy Barker, Thornton-Cleveleys

At Wootton Bassett, near Swindon, in October 1940, a party of about thirty Pioneers were on detachment. Our duties were to work with the Royal Engineers in the erection of a Nissen hut camp. One dark morning when we paraded at about 8 a.m. in our denims and general working gear, the NCO proceeded to go through the ranks, shining a torch in our faces, and also at our feet. I think at least half the detachment was found not to have shaved, or to have had dirty boots.

All the unfortunates were ordered to parade at 6.30 p.m. at the company office in their best suits and smartened up. Everything went quite well, until one tall young man was discovered without his gaiters.

'Where's your gaiters, man?' asked the NCO. 'You'll be coming on parade in a bloody high hat next!'

Leslie Randall, Lambeth

On an anti-aircraft gun site somewhere in England, a sentry is patrolling. An extra duty is for him to answer the telephone when it rings a 'red alert', which means that enemy planes are approaching. As he patrols, he hears footsteps coming up the lonely, dark country lane. He rises to the big occasion with a sharp 'Halt, who goes there? Friend or foe?'

It is an orderly sergeant and an orderly officer making a tour of inspection. The orderly sergeant answers: 'Friend.'

At this precise moment, the telephone rings and the sentry says to the orderly sergeant: 'Hold this a moment, will you?' and hands him his rifle.

The sergeant cannot believe his ears, but takes the rifle. The sentry picks up the phone and takes the message, then returns to the waiting sergeant and as-yet unidentified officer, takes the rifle back and says: 'Thanks, sergeant, pass friend, all is well!'

And the officer is permitted to accompany the sergeant without being challenged, or shot as a foe!

C. Clark, Maidstone

We'd been out on the assault course and were dead beat. We returned to our Nissen hut and stoked up the fire in the stove that stood in the centre of the hut. We hung our denims all around to dry, then turned in. The stove heated up and the chimney glowed red. A pair of denims caught alight. A Corporal Diamond called out the fire picket. They told him to get stuffed. Everyone just lay on their beds. So he ran out to get the fire bucket. The roof was blazing at this point but no one else moved. He came back with the bucket, looked down at his mud-stained feet and, before throwing it on the fire, sat on the end of a bed and washed his feet!

Roy Barker, Thornton-Cleveleys

A cockney lance corporal was becoming annoyed with a certain private. Wagging a finger at him, he said: 'I'll put you on a charge for insubordination. I don't know how to spell it, but I'll soon find out.'

Leslie Randall, Lambeth

I was in the ack-ack from 1940 to 1946 and moved around quite a bit from Wales, Scotland, the London area and quite a few others. I recall being stationed at Wick. Our camp was quite near to the Ross Head Lighthouse and to get there we had to pass through Wick airfield, which was run by the RAF, and along a lonely country road. One very dark night, the sentry on the gate heard this 'clip-clop' coming along the road and as it got nearer and nearer, he could just make out a white patch. He was scared out of his wits. It turned out to be one of our chaps returning to camp from local leave. He'd had quite a few drinks and had borrowed a horse from a field. He rode it into camp and even tried to get it up the steps into the guardroom. There was pandemonium.

Ernest Bamforth, Lincoln

Snoring has always been a topic of conversation in my life, whenever sleep is mentioned. I suppose I could claim to be 'the greatest'.

It came to a head one night in 1941. Sleeping in one of the barrack rooms with about thirty other soldiers, I must have excelled myself with extra loud snores and grunts. Tin hats had been thrown at me, some missed, others, alas, were on target. Heavy boots also came my way with the same results. Nothing, it seemed, would wake me up and halt the snoring. So my bunkmates pulled me out of bed, stripped me starkers and lay me on the floor in the freezing cold.

In the morning that's how the sergeant found me on his 'wakey-wakey' tour. Sore and black and blue, teeth chattering, I had a terrible job explaining what had happened. One of the lads came to my rescue and told him the story. But I had the last laugh – the MO gave me 'excused duties' for that day.

F. G. Jones, *Shotton, Deeside*

The army had taken over a new housing estate in Liverpool for the purpose of billeting recruits, of whom I was one. Can you imagine my feelings when the house I was seconded to contained the heavyweight boxing champion Larry Gains, the Fielding Brothers – themselves two well-known pugilists, and a PT instructor named Fred Fulwood who was the local strongman from the same street as me? And I, of all things, worked as a window dresser. What a mixture! Naturally I was proud to live in the same billet as such a famous hero as Larry Gains. Alas, he wasn't the most humorous of persons, probably his career had contributed to that. As I walked up the bare stairs in my heavy boots that first night, I was greeted by the great man himself, who roared: 'Take those bloody boots off when you walk up and down the stairs!'

Needless to say, from then onwards, off came those boots!

F. G. Jones, Shotton, Deeside

Officer: Well, young man, what were you before you were called up for the army?
New recruit: 'Appy, Sir!

P. H. LEWIS, BRIDGEND, GLAMORGAN

The orderly officer on his rounds walked into our mess at dinner and asked the same old question: 'Any complaints?'

One soldier replied: 'Yes, sir. We can't eat this meat. It's so bad that a dog wouldn't eat it.'

Well, the officer happened to have his dog with him and picked up a piece of the meat and threw it at the dog. The dog just swallowed it and the officer, eyebrow raised, said: 'It must be all right.'

The officer walked on. The dog hung back.

The soldier called after the officer: 'Look at your dog now! He's licking his arse to get the taste out of his mouth!'

Mr S. E. Smith, Essex

I was in the Royal Engineers at Thorpe Mill, Triangle, near Halifax in 1942. We would parade every morning on the square and the lieutenant colonel would stand at the end of the parade ground, always accompanied by his Alsatian dog.

We always said that dog ate ten men's rations. One morning we were all lined up and Sergeant Major Henry Hall, complete with silver-knobbed stick, bawled out to the entire parade: 'Ah-ten . . .' an order which the Alsatian finished with a mighty 'Woof!'

Every man stood sharply to attention and then fell into roars of laughter as we realized we had been brought to attention by a dog. The lieutenant colonel turned away to conceal a laugh but the sergeant major went barmy, all red in the face and shouting: 'As you were!'

I think that's the only time the Royal Engineers were brought smartly up by a dog.

Mr A. S. Cobb, Hull

I was stationed at Cleave AA camp near Bude. The warrant officers and sergeants were accommodated in huts with separate rooms, each of which was shared by two men. One night when two of the sergeants were in the mess bar, a sheep, which had been grazing nearby, was caught and put into their room. The electric lamp was removed and the door closed. Later that night, the sergeants, having consumed a few beers, returned to their room. You can imagine the rumpus. The sheep was running around the room trying to get out, and neither of the sergeants had a clue what was happening.

W. Norris, Watford

It was 1941 and I was serving 'somewhere in the south of England'. Our day began with a forty-mile route march. It was customary, as I remember, to have a five- or ten-minute break after every hour. On our first stop the first priority was to relieve ourselves. Over the wall we leapt and into the woods. Imagine our surprise when the young saplings, plus a number of small bushes, began to move in all directions. We had disturbed a bunch of soldiers on manoeuvres. They were certainly perfectly camouflaged!

F. G. Jones, Shotton, Deeside

A comrade of mine related a tale of when he was in the Royal Artillery. He had been on an AA gun site. One day they were inspected by a general and the gunner had been detailed to stand by the Lewis gun, in a sandbagged pit. The general made his way around the site, having a word here and there. When he got to the gunner, he exchanged small talk. He asked him how long he had been in the army and then his attention turned to his training.

'If you were to see a German plane coming in low to attack this site, would you open fire on your own, or wait for the order?'

'Neither,' said the gunner, 'I'd get laid down at the back of the sandbags because I've got no ammunition!'

Poor Gunner Hawkins spent the next two months beside that gun!

Mr A. S. Cobb, Hull

A young junior officer was made orderly officer for the day. Making his inspection, he went to the cookhouse to inspect the cooking. Looking into one pan he noticed that it was boiling around the edges, but not in the middle. He asked the cook to explain this.

'That bit's for the sentries, sir. We always serve them first!'

MR S. E. SMITH, ESSEX

Some of my best times in the army happened while stationed in the Orkneys. To fill in time we had various half-hour lectures, one concerning 'Demob'. Various conditions as to how, and when, we might be demobbed, were discussed – things like length of service, overseas duty, war wounds, married men with dependents etc. But the climax came when one cockney voice piped up from the rear: 'As long as they don't do it in bleedin' alphabetical order!'

His name, you see, was Gunner Tom Zelkin!

Clifford Bailey, Dudley

Walking down the main street of my hometown while on leave, I approached a crossroads and spotted a large car approaching with the Duke of Kent inside. Being in uniform, and with my rifle slung over my shoulder, I wasn't sure what kind of salute to give and had precious little time to make my mind up. I attempted to give a butt salute. Wearing heavy army boots didn't help. I tried to halt at the kerb, slipped on my back and up in the air went my rifle, missing the royal car by inches. What a laugh His Highness must have had. And what a scramble I made!

F. G. Jones, Shotton, Deeside

The place was Blackdown training camp. The year was 1940. Our squad was being trained as gunners or drivers in the Royal Artillery. One day in the gym we had to climb ropes, tumble on mats and jump over the vaulting horse. One cockney, named Joe Brown, was hopeless at PT, so each time he had to jump the vaulting horse he would pretend to tie up his shoelaces and miss his turn. Eventually, the sergeant spotted this and yelled: 'Hey, you! Over the horse!'

Joe replied: 'I don't mind being a gunner, don't mind being a driver, but I ain't going to be a bleeding acrobat for two bob a day!'

H. Walls, Highams Park, London

During the war we were stationed at a place for training and living under canvas. Most of the chaps were a happy-go-lucky bunch and shared alike. That is, if one had cakes or a cake sent, they shared it with their mates in the tent. Anyhow, in my tent we had one very tight-fisted bloke. Now this particular afternoon the post clerk came and gave him a parcel. Most of the chaps were either writing letters or cleaning up. We all waited in anticipation and behold – out came a homemade fruit cake and a large pot of strawberry jam. Now, he cut a slice of cake for himself, put the rest of it back in the box. To make it worse, he kept going on about this cake and, eventually, I got very cross and told him: 'If you don't shut up about that damned cake, I'll come over there and wrap it around your neck!'

The NCO in the tent told us to 'pack it up' and the incident passed. Teatime came and as we filed into the dining room, lo and behold, there was this chap with his knapsack. Out came the cake and the jam. But then he dropped his knife and as he climbed under the table to retrieve it, I grabbed the jam and passed it down the tables to my comrades. When he came back up and realized the jam was gone, he looked straight at me. At that exact moment, the orderly officer and sergeant were making their rounds. When we were asked if we had any complaints, the tight-fist said: 'Yes, sir. Woodham has pinched my pot of strawberry jam!'

'Have you got his jam, Woodham?' said the officer with a big grin.

'No, sir!' I said.

The sergeant was about to burst and the officer said: 'Put this man [the tight-fist] on extra weekend guard for making a frivolous complaint!'

The tight-fist complained that this particular weekend he had a pass, but the sergeant told him that unless he could get someone to stand in for him, his leave would be cancelled.

He had a special occasion lined up, it seemed, and he was desperate to be able to use his pass so he came into the tent trying to persuade someone to stand in for him. There were no takers. Then he offered me five shillings to do it and I said: 'Not on your Nelly! Make it ten shillings and we'll go to the RSM and sort it out!'

The RSM agreed to postpone his duty until the next weekend and, as we were leaving, he called me back.

'How much did that cost him?'

'Ten shillings,' I replied.

'Not bad!' said the RSM.

A good result all-round, but I never did find out what happened to that pot of jam!

Mr A. E. Woodham, Slough

We were stationed at Chesterfield. On our evenings off, we stood about on the street corners, doing nothing particular, only to be moved on by the MPs, or Redcaps as they were better known. By September 1941, my mate and I had a medical board and were eventually discharged. Awaiting the usual formalities – train tickets, coupons for civvy clothes – we decided to take a last stroll through the town, minus cap, no gaiters, jacket undone and hands in our pockets. We walked straight into the arms of two Redcaps. We decided to pull their legs, refusing to button up our tunics and not standing to attention. Eventually we showed them our discharge certificates and to their credit they took it in good part and actually shook our hands, wishing us the best of luck.

F. G. Jones, Shotton, Deeside

While I was waiting for my demob group to come up, I was sent from my depot at Lowestoft to a small naval overflow camp at Hopton-on-Sea that, before and after the war, was a holiday camp. I was caught for colour guard. The camp had no band, so for ceremonial occasions we had to rely on a gramophone record. We were fell-in on a parade, some 500 or so, then brought to attention and given the order: 'Royal salute, present arms.' But instead of the strains of the national anthem coming over the tannoy, all we got was Judy Garland singing 'The Trolley Song' complete with clanging bells! Five hundred men burst out laughing.

The offending signalman, who had put on the wrong record, doubled-up to the commander. The officer asked him if he knew how far it was around the football field. When the signalman said that, no, he didn't know, the officer told him: 'Well bloody well find out – and don't come back!'

Mr R. Taylor, Hull

When I was in the cookhouse we always made the custard for the duff with water, it never saw milk. One day, as we prepared to dish up dinner, there was a panic. We had no hot water to make the custard. So one 'gastronomic genius' suggested straining the water from the carrots and using that. What a row we had with the lads when they got custard with tiny bits of carrot in it. We tried to tell them it was little bits of peaches, but they weren't fooled.

Mr A. S. Cobb, Hull

During the early part of the war, I was a lieutenant in a unit stationed in Bradford. Our colonel had arranged for the officers to attend a variety show on the Saturday evening. I was due to be orderly officer the next day. A well-known Bradford socialite had also laid on a party for us at her home and so it was arranged that we would go there immediately after the variety show was over. At the latter, one of the acts was a race across the stage on little wooden rocking horses. According to how they were jerked forward, they either went along or just collapsed and the rider had to pick himself up and start again. The chorus girls gave a trial run and then called for volunteers to go up on the stage and take a horse each. Well, before we knew where we were, a lieutenant friend and I found ourselves manhandled up onto the stage to take part. There we were in all our glory, full service dress and Sam Brownes, falling off the horses!

When the show was over, it was nearly 11 p.m. and off we went to the party. This went on until about 8 a.m., but I left at 6.30 a.m. as I had to inspect the men's billets and then the breakfast, besides cleaning myself up. I then had to take church parade. As I'd had no rest for over twenty-four hours, you can imagine how I felt. I just managed to reach the church with the unit in fair regimental order. But the moment I sat in the pew, I just fell fast asleep. The colonel was reading the lesson and, exactly as he finished, my friend nudged me awake. Now, in that split second of waking, I was still in the theatre and, in the deathly silence of the church, I started clapping loudly and must have got in about five to six claps before I realized. You can imagine the reaction of the troops. No act at the theatre the night before got half such a hilarious reception as I received.

Later that afternoon my friend and I were told to report to the colonel's HQ at 10 a.m. the following day. I was called in first and the colonel really let me have it over making a fool of myself at the theatre. Then he came to the church incident. This was beyond description! I just wanted to drop dead. My friend, who followed, only got the theatre fiasco.

About eighteen months later, while serving in Egypt, I was spending seven days' leave at Shepheard's Hotel in Cairo. One morning, as I was leaving the hotel, I passed my old colonel and a brigadier. I gave them a super salute and walked on. But I had only gone a few steps when a voice called out: 'Captain?'

I turned around and the colonel beckoned me over.

'Weren't you once in a unit that I commanded?'

I said: 'Yes, sir. In Bradford.'

'Good! Now we can prove it! I've told the story so many times and to so many, and I know that few have believed me!'

He then told me to go back into the hotel, where I was taken to the cocktail bar. About two hours later, a rather tottery brigadier, a not-too-good colonel and a very sickly me, parted ways.

Reg C. Coutanche, Bournemouth

When serving in the Royal Welch Fusiliers in 1942 (70th Battalion Young Soldiers Regiment), we had a march to a firing range a few miles away. Before bivouacking overnight, we were allowed to go to the village, but the OC ordered that full corporals and ranks above, including all officers, drink at one pub and lance corporals and fusiliers at the other. This was typical of the OC, a stuffy sort of bloke, and, of course, such class distinction was entirely out of place in the circumstances.

So, we were having a drink in one of the pubs (I was a full corporal) and the officers were in the best room. My mate 'Yob' Yardley, a lancejack who lived in Blackpool, came to the door of the pub and asked for me, and asked if I could get him any fags, which of course were not always available, especially to strangers. We had each been sold five in this particular pub, so I asked the landlady if she could spare five more for my friend. Suspicious that I was trying to get another 'ration' for myself, she asked why my friend couldn't ask for them himself.

I explained, quite innocently, that he was not allowed to come into the pub and why – and then the fat really hit the fire! Whether she was a socialist, or whether the fact that the far greater proportion of the company were spending their money at the other pub, motivated her, I don't know, but she flounced into the best room and turned the officers out and they had to finish their beers outside. I, of course, made myself really scarce, although I was pleased at the outcome!

Les Sutton, Manchester

While training at the depot of the Royal Scots, outside Edinburgh, just after the fall of France, one night in the NAAFI, I overheard a Scottish soldier comment: 'This'll be a long war if the English pack in.'

W. ABBOTT, LONDON

I'm five feet two inches tall and weigh eight stone four pounds. Not exactly a Hercules! Being in the Royal Artillery, we were sent to Northern Ireland to defend an aerodrome not far from the Loch Erne Hotel. One windy night I was perched in a sentry box on a hill, with respirator covering my chest, rifle on my shoulder with fixed bayonet, complete with helmet. Every few minutes the sentry box gave a lurch. Suddenly a strong gust blew the box, with me inside it, down into some bushes and the box fell with the opening towards the ground. I was trapped, good and proper. I could not move the flipping box, everything was on top of me. The bayonet snapped off and the rifle was making love to me while the respirator had fallen between my shoulder blades. I shouted like a football hooligan for help, but the box drowned out my frantic cries. When the gunner due to relieve me couldn't find me, he called out the guard and they finally found me in the bushes.

It took five gunners, with ropes, to get the box, with me inside, free. I landed up in military hospital in Belfast with a badly bruised face and no sympathy. Everyone thought it was frightfully funny!

Henry Doll, Croydon

One soldier elected to serve on the messing committee but didn't know anything about food. So when he went on leave, he asked his wife for ideas. She told him to ask for Scotch eggs. Next time we met it was agreed that Scotch eggs would be on the menu for tea one evening. When his turn came to be served, he looked at it and said: 'Blimey, that's only half an egg! Where's the other half?'

S. E. Smith, Dovercourt, Essex

The RSM Grenadier Guards had been in the gas chamber testing his mask. He told the troops to put their fingers inside the mask and have a quick whiff so that they would know what the gas really smells like. Unfortunately, his own whiff was too much. His eyes filled with water and he bent down. I touched him on the shoulder and said: 'Don't cry, Sergeant Major! The war will soon be over!'

Mr B. Croft, Stafford

Scene: Recruiting office.
'What's your name, number one?'
'Potts, sir.'
'What's your name, number two?'
'Philpotts, sir.'
'I suppose you will be teapots, number three?'
'No, sir, Chambers!'

R. HERRINGTON

It was July 1945, and I was one of a party of men from Group 9 who were going to Queen Elizabeth Barracks in York to give up our arms and equipment, prior to demob or release. We were a very motley crowd – warrant officers, junior and senior NCOs and privates. In fact, we had more stripes among us than would be found in a safari park full of zebras! We were met at the railway station by a very junior lance corporal who was to be our guide. He ordered us to 'sling arms and march at ease'. This we did and wended our way.

When getting near to our destination, we saw two small boy cadets sitting on a fence. As we passed them, one of the youngsters said to his friend: 'Blimey, look at this scruffy lot!'

His companion replied: 'Sshh! Some of these are old Dunkirk men!'

Unabashed, the first lad replied: 'Blimey, did we have to depend on them?'

Charles Isles, Newton Abbott

A young American army officer was running along the platform at Paddington Station, looking for a seat in a train. When hearing the warning of imminent departure, he pushed his way into a crowded compartment. All the seats were occupied, including one by a dog. Attempting to displace the dog, he was interrupted by a frosty-faced lady who told him: 'The dog belongs to a friend who has gone to the ladies' lavatory on the platform and it is keeping her seat for her.' Just then the train began to move. The American remarked: 'Your friend is missing the train and will want her dog!'

He then promptly thrust the dog through the window and took the seat. Whereupon a British army colonel, opposite, took his nose out of his newspaper, speared the American with a basilisk eye and growled: 'You Yanks do everything the wrong way! You drive on the wrong side of the road, eat your food with the fork in the wrong hand, and now you have dropped the wrong bitch out of the window!'

J. A. Hawkins, Buckfastleigh, Devon

My brother was a major in the RASC. He and his men were sent on the hazardous mission of burying boxes of ammunition on the enemy beach, to be used by the men who were to make the raid on Dieppe. They duly buried the marked boxes. However, when the survivors returned, my brother learned that one box, marked 'Bren Gun Ammo', in fact contained thousands of loose false teeth.

An investigation revealed that an army dental depot had reported losing a box marked in just that way but which in fact was used to store single dentures.

He could only say that the next time they stored teeth in this way, they should make them into full sets. At least the invaders could bite the Germans to death.

Mrs C. Murphy, Rotherham

In 1942, I did my first six weeks' training at Sowerby Bridge. Then, us soldiers destined for the Royal Signals had to stay in a large unused warehouse, ready for transport to Folkestone for nine months' signals training. This particular evening, about one hundred of us rookies got together talking and, to my surprise, I found three other men who, like me, worked for the Gas, Light and Coke Company and were all fitters. We had much in common. Suddenly, in came the sergeant and said: 'You lot – get a bed for tonight and shut up!'

The four of us went to the end beds and I took the fourth from the wall. During the night the NAAFI was broken into and thousands of cigarettes were stolen. We were all suspects and, first thing next morning, it was: 'Stand by your beds and bring out your kitbags!'

Nothing was found, so the sergeant said: 'Right, we'll question you all separately.'

The sergeant and two civilian police, trilby hats, pencils and pads at the ready, picked our corner in which to start. The sergeant asked the questions – name, service number, home address and occupation. Number one interviewee answered them all, finishing with his occupation: 'Gas fitter, Gas, Light and Coke Company.'

Number two gave his answers and, of course, the same occupation. The trio looked at one another, but said nothing. When number three gave the same answer – 'Gas fitter, Gas, Light and Coke Company' – the sergeant and his colleagues weren't amused.

Now it was my turn. This time, one of the detectives asked the questions. When he got to 'occupation', he was clearly irritated: 'Now, go on! Say you're a bloody gas fitter and work for the bloody Gas, Light and Coke Company!'

In a low voice I replied: 'Well, actually, yes, I do!'

The warehouse exploded with delight. The detective threw his pencil and pad on the floor and jumped on them.

He shouted at the rest: 'If any more of you claim to be gas fitters with the Gas, Light and Coke Company, we'll have to start again.' It was quite a job to convince them that the lot of us hadn't got together and decided to become gas fitters that morning.

H. Walters, Southend-on-Sea

I was called up into the Royal Artillery (searchlights), probably as a judgement on me for taking the mickey out of them during the pre-war training, as they never seemed to get anything in the beam. What a boring life! There were some characters, though, and I'll never forget them.

We had a young Londoner who was very dim and talked through his teeth. I say he was dim. Before the war he'd been a bookie's runner and he could tell you how much was due to you for a shilling each way if you won at odds of 31–7.

Anyway, one morning the NCO detailed him to fill all the hurricane lamps with paraffin. Off he went, but soon came back and said he couldn't do it because there was no paraffin. The NCO said: 'Quite correct, but the paraffin is being delivered this afternoon. Until then, go around the site and clean all the glasses.'

Our friend thought very hard for a moment – always a dangerous thing for him – then replied: 'OK, but it won't take me very long. I can only think of two men on the site who wear glasses.'

A. J. Johnson, Solihull

Between 1941 and 1943 I was stationed near Thurso, Caithness, in the very north of Scotland. During the worst of one terrible winter, with several inches of snow on the ground, I was transferred to Brechin. There were huge delays on the railway line and it took me hours to get through to my new posting. An officer welcomed me and said that I'd done very well just to get there. When he checked my papers he was astonished to find that I hadn't had any leave for about a year, so I was given a week's leave and set off on a really difficult journey to Derby and the wife I hadn't seen for a year.

It took me about twenty-four hours to make the trip through the snow, and when I finally arrived there was a telegram waiting for me. I was being called back to Brechin immediately. So I travelled back to Brechin – it was another very long trip and some trains had to be dug out of the snow – and reported for duty, whereupon I was told that my unit, stationed near Thurso, had called me back. So I went back there, again experiencing all the vagaries of the Scottish weather and more delays, and eventually reported to my original commanding officer.

'Yes,' the officer said, 'the reason we've called you back is that we've been looking at your records and we see that you haven't had any leave for over a year. Why don't you take a week's leave and report back to us before going to Brechin?' So I set off for Derby again. I was travelling the best part of the week, and I never did go to Brechin. I returned to my original unit and remained with them.

Tim Ward, Barton under Needwood, Staffordshire

I managed to get on an intensive course on radar at Blackpool Tech. There were about 110 of us altogether and we were a motley lot. Every Friday morning we paraded right along the front at Blackpool. This was a sight to be believed as we were chosen for our educational record, rather than for our soldierliness! The full sergeant in charge used to take us and one Friday he told us he'd had enough. We must do better or else. He boomed: 'Hold your heads up, swing your arms – and look ahead. No point in looking down. They're too bloody mean in Blackpool to leave threepenny bits in the gutter!'

A. J. Johnson, Solihull

Sam Weller – his parents may have been fans of Charles Dickens – was an airman stationed at Diamond Harbour, near Calcutta. A mysterious tropical illness had left him completely bald with, quite literally, not a hair on his head. Eventually he was issued with a service wig, whispy, stringy and straggly. On his first day off after acquiring the wig, Weller went into Calcutta in his best starched bush jacket, slacks and solar pith helmet. Walking down a busy main street thronged with fellow servicemen, he felt a tap on his shoulder.

Turning, he was confronted by a military policeman who snapped: 'Airman, haircut, you.'

Weller swept off his helmet with one hand, his wig with the other, to reveal a bald head glinting in the sunshine.

'Oh, so you think so?' he replied.

A. F. Dawn, Derby

I was travelling north on a train full of soldiers and we were approaching Preston. Trains almost always stopped for several minutes at Preston and there was a great place for tea if you were quick – but if you weren't quick you'd never get served. As the train came into Preston station, it slowed down to stop. One soldier was standing right by the door. His boots were already off but he took tea orders from two or three others and hopped off the train as it rolled to a stop. He sprinted for the tea stall in his socks. He'd gone about ten paces when the train suddenly, surprisingly, picked up pace again and headed north. The soldier on the platform stopped running and looked back in horror as everybody shouted through the window at him: 'Keep mine warm until I get back' and 'Extra sugar in mine.'

Tim Ward, Barton under Needwood, Staffordshire

I had a spell at Catterick and we were in huts built about fifty years earlier. They had been designed to sleep about eighteen men, but since we were in double bunks they now housed around sixty. So with blackouts in place, the atmosphere was rather overpowering to say the least.

In the still of the night, one of the chaps broke wind rather noisily. His bedfellow on the top bunk rebuked him and said: 'What do you want to do that for? It's bad enough in here anyway!'

His mate replied: 'What are you beefing about? You have to fart in here for a breath of fresh air!'

A. J. Johnson, Solihull

I was a Japanese POW sent to help build a runway on the outskirts of Makassar on the island of Celebes. During the *yasmi* – rest period – one of the lads came across a hoard of toilet soap in a Jap hut and promptly secreted a bar away in a little pouch which he had suspended under his crotch, hoping to beat the inevitable search when we arrived back at camp. On the way back it began to rain – one of those typical torrential downpours in the Far East – and we were ordered to 'run, run . . . quicklee'. The faster he ran, the more luxurious the lather produced by the friction of the soldier's legs. It was the whitest of white trails ever blazed in the Far East.

William Climie, London

The scene was a seaside villa near Catalina in Sicily and men of 2 Troop (Heavy Weapons Section), 3 Commando had just returned from a raid on the Italian mainland. Even after this traumatic experience the commandos still had one chore to complete: a weapons inspection by a young second lieutenant.

When the officer reached Ginger Hodgson, a tough Yorkshireman from Leeds, he was offered Hodgson's Colt .45 pistol.

'Bad barrel, Hodgson,' said the young officer in a disapproving voice.

'Yes sir,' barked Hodgson, '. . . in the sea at Vaago, sir!'

He was referring to a famous commando raid which took place in Norway in December 1941.

'Oh I see,' said the officer and continued down the ranks as the men behind him sniggered.

Moments later the penny dropped: 'Wait a minute, Hodgson, you weren't at Vaago.'

'No sir, I wasn't. But the pistol was.'

Frank Smith, Luton

An RAF corporal had just taken a commission and, as is the usual custom, was due to be transferred to another unit. Before his posting, however, he was given the task of orderly officer on the day following his being granted his commission. During his tour of the dining hall at breakfast time, he stopped beside another corporal and asked the usual question: 'Any complaints?'

The corporal looked up from his meal and answered with a wry grin: 'You damn well know there are: you were sitting here yourself yesterday!'

Silently the new officer, now with a red face, and the orderly sergeant, with a sly grin, moved on.

Mr R. Munday, Gravesend, Essex

In the week leading to D-Day, I was serving as an eighteen-year-old ordinary seaman on the light cruiser HMS *Scylla*. We were all keyed-up awaiting the great day when we would sail across the Channel to begin the invasion. The ship would put to sea most evenings on exercises and most days we would be at anchor outside Portsmouth Harbour. Our days at anchor were spent keeping the ship in readiness for battle, and on one of these days I was detailed to paint part of the superstructure behind the forward funnel. The colour of the paint was, of course, battleship grey. The main object for me to paint was a vent that carried stale air from a compartment below deck. The top of this vent had a stout wire mesh to stop objects falling into the compartment below. A heavy lid on a hinge was at right angles to the opening, which would be closed and battened down at sea to act as a blackout and also to stop sea-spray entering.

I had painted the air vent and had started on the lid, putting the gallon paint tin on the wire mesh so that I could reach it with the brush. Eventually I came to a very hard-to-reach part that involved me getting myself in a very awkward position. In my eagerness to complete the task, I lifted the catch holding the heavy lid upright to paint behind it. The lid closed with a very heavy bang and, while still using the last brushful of paint, I was confronted with a terrible sight.

In front of me stood the chief cook, covered from head to toe in a mixture of custard and battleship-grey paint. His face, including his beard, unrecognizable under this mess. It suddenly dawned on me what I had done. On closing the lid, I had forgotten that the paint tin was beneath it. As the lid slammed down, it smashed the tin through the wire mesh, sending it falling at least twenty feet into a large vat of hot custard being made ready for lunch in the galley below.

The chief cook and some of his staff, all of whom happened to be standing near the vat, were covered in this mixture of custard and paint. Awaiting a burst of anger and having visions of spending weeks in detention quarters, I gazed at the paint-covered cook. After what seemed like an eternity, and to my great relief, the chief cook burst out in a fit of laughter and beckoned me to follow him to view the devastation below. Still laughing, he showed me the galley covered in the slime and when I offered to help clean up, he advised me to get to the other end of the ship when painting in future.

Needless to say, the news quickly spread throughout the crew and no one had an appetite for custard with their pudding that day. I was immediately christened 'the Custard King' and was subject to good-natured banter for days afterwards.

William Foulds, Haslingden, Lancashire

I was in the merchant navy and served on several ships belonging to various companies. One of these was of the T & J Harrison 'Hungry Harrison' Line of Liverpool. As the nickname implies, rations were of the minimum and when, as often happened, we had to sail off-course because of suspected raiders in the vicinity, they grew even less.

On one occasion, a grumbling able seaman said: 'On every other ship after two or three weeks at sea, I always dream about luscious women. On this one, all I dream of is pork chops!'

Things got so bad that a delegation went to see the captain, taking with them a tray of food. Eight men asked whether it was right that they should have such meals. Thinking that they were complaining about the quality rather than quantity, the captain picked up a knife and fork and tucked in. When the plate was clean he looked up and said, triumphantly: 'There was nothing wrong with that, was there?'

'Maybe not, sir,' came the reply, 'but that there food was for the whole ruddy watch!'

Kenneth S. Allen, Northwood, Middlesex

In 1944, I was at the School of Technical Training at RAF Locking. Every Thursday was what the officers called 'Domestic Evening', although the rest of us called it 'bull night'. Each airman had to polish his bed space and this polishing got to such a fine art that we used to tie pieces of rag under our boots to help polish the floor and avoid making any scratch marks.

On Friday when we were in the workshops, the CO and his retinue, consisting of adjutant, flight lieutenant, station warrant officer, flight sergeant, orderly sergeant and, bringing up the rear, the hut corporal, did the inspection. When we got back to the hut at lunchtime, there, pinned to the table, was a note that read: 'The occupiers of this hut will stay in tonight and re-clean it.'

Everyone in the forces knows that you obey the last order, and argue for 'redress of grievance' afterwards. So, after tea, we got stuck in and cleaned the hut again, without much enthusiasm. Eventually we collared the corporal and asked which part of the hut was causing the problem. We thought it was as clean as most others and better than many that had not had to be re-cleaned.

After a while the corporal said: 'Just get on and clean everything. I'm not having the CO come in here and saying again, for everyone to hear, that this hut is beyond reproach.' I don't think that a hut corporal had ever got so close to being murdered.

George Godfrey, Bridgend

Corporal to new squad: Is there a clerk here?
Bloke next to me says: Yes, Corporal.
Corporal: Right, you will be in charge of laundry packages.
Bloke to his mate: Why pick on me?
Mate: You volunteered, didn't you?
Bloke: No, my name is Clark.

D. B. CURRAH, NEWQUAY

When a baby arrives in the family of a crew member, it is the custom, if the ship is in a home port, for the baby to be named on board, in the presence of the ship's company. If acceptable to the parents, it is traditional to bestow the name of the ship on the child – 'Penelope' for example. But, of course, not all parents wish to do this, and often have deep family reasons for making an alternative choice.

Chief Petty Officer Henry Chew and his wife duly presented themselves, complete with infant, on the quarterdeck of the ship at the appointed time. They handed over the baby to the tender arms of the ship's padre.

With the child held correctly and firmly in his left arm, he dipped his right hand into the waters of the font, turned to the parents and, with due ceremony, asked them: 'What is the chosen name for the child?'

The Chews replied: 'Iris.'

Padre: 'And the second name of the child?'

Parents: 'Elizabeth, sir, after our dear queen.'

The padre dipped his hand into the waters of the font, made the traditional mark on the child's forehead and said: 'I herewith name this child Elizabeth, by which name she shall forthwith be always known.'

After the ceremony, as the more informal type of wetting the baby's head took place, the padre was asked why on earth he had neglected to name the baby 'Iris'. After all, there were expectations from an elderly aunt of that name.

The padre came straight to the point and said: 'You are used to your surname, I don't doubt. But I would have felt very sorry indeed for you, as the child's parents, when she grew up and got her own back on you for the leg-pulling she would undoubtedly have suffered at school with a name like "Iris Chew".'

T. H. Gibbs-Murray, Greenwich

During a weekend break, I was staying at RAF Long Kesh, which later became the Maze prison. We stayed there while our ship was being repaired, after slight damage, in Belfast dockyards.

On the Saturday morning, five of us visited the YMCA and, it not yet being opening time in the pubs, we decided to visit the riding school we had seen advertised in the YMCA. It was in a posh part of Belfast and, when we mounted our horses, folks came out into the street to see us. Almost every house had at least one person looking out from a window at the peculiar site of a bunch of sailors in uniform, riding horses.

George Harris, Dudley

Leading Seaman Frank Wilson, known as 'Tug', put in his request to the ship's captain for compassionate leave to visit his wife for the arrival of their first child.

'Negative!' came the response. 'Your presence was, no doubt absolutely essential at the laying of the keel, but not, repeat not, at the launching.'

T. H. Gibbs-Murray, Greenwich

My brother had quite a colourful war career. At one point he trained with the SAS. In Cyprus, his group raided an island and took a top-brass enemy officer, as well as the driver of a big Mercedes, captive. They left with their targets and placed a note on the windscreen of the car: 'Sorry, we have no use for the car.'

Gladys Lutterloch, Yeovil

My husband told a tale of the day he went for his medical, just after he joined up. He was very concerned because he would be facing a woman doctor. So he reluctantly lined up with the others, all of whom, like he, were 'starkers'. But that doctor cut through all the embarrassment when she asked: 'Does someone's mother use Persil?' When my husband looked around, he realized that his very naked, very white body was lined up between two strapping black men.

Mrs C. G. Atkins, Bourne, Buckinghamshire

My brother served in the Western Desert. He had been working on tank maintenance and was taking a break so that his comrade could take a photograph of him proudly showing off his lovely new red beard. Suddenly an enemy aircraft was sighted and started to drop 'eggs' as he called them, and blasted off low-level cannon fire.

They dived for cover under the nearest vehicle, all of which were draped in camouflage netting to avoid enemy detection. When the plane was eventually chased off, they emerged only to discover that they had been sheltering under an ammo truck.

Gladys Lutterloch, Yeovil

I was in the RAF and we were playing a football match at Uxbridge. I was taking a corner when suddenly there was this huge explosion. Everybody, including their goalkeeper, threw themselves to the ground and the ball sailed straight into the empty net, or at least it must have done because when we all got up again, there it lay. The explosion hadn't been caused by enemy action but by the UXB boys detonating a landmine. I would claim that I scored the only landmine-assisted goal in the history of football, but the rotten referee made me take the corner again.

Cardew Robinson, Twickenham St Margarets

I was on leave with my mate from the same town, and after we'd got off the train we decided to call into the nearest pub for a couple of pints before going home. The landlord hadn't even got time to pull our pints before the air-raid warning siren went off and everyone, including mine host, dashed out for the shelter, which was a public one in the street. He didn't even bother to lock up and we just sat there. Well, my mate looked at me, and I looked at him, and I think it crossed both our minds that we could lean over the bar and pull our own beer. But we did the decent thing because we weren't dishonest men. We just drank up everyone else's beer that they'd left on the bar and various tables. Then we shot off. As a matter of fact, there wasn't a raid but I often wonder what those other customers must have thought when then they came back into the pub after the all-clear sounded, and found that all their drinks had disappeared. Just empty glasses left. Needless to say that we didn't use that pub again. Also needless to say, I'd prefer it if you didn't put my name to this.

Anonymous, Chester

In 1945 I was in the RAF. The war, by then, was going well and we had the Nazis on the run. One day, someone posted a notice that read: 'If aircraft in camouflage markings are spotted, it will be the RAF. If aircraft painted silver are spotted, it will be the USAAF. If no aircraft are spotted, it will be the Luftwaffe.'

Roy Burns, Derbyshire

I was employed as an electrician to the War Department. The commanding officer at one camp where I was stationed was walking around with four other 'brass hats'. As he passed me, he said: 'Hello, sparks! How is the world treating you?'

I replied: 'Very seldom, sir, very seldom!'

And they all laughed at that.

Later, I had a wiring job in the quartermaster's stores where they were kitting out a newcomer to the ranks with a new battle dress. The conversation went something like this:

'How's the blouse?'

'Okay.'

'How's the trousers?'

'Okay.'

'Blimey, we've got a ruddy cripple here!'

There were only two sizes, you see – too big and too small.

Another time I was working at a German POW camp when a grey-haired German told me that he was an electrician and that he used to have his own electrical business. I asked him what he meant by 'used to have'.

He just shrugged: 'Along come RAF. Poof! No business!'

W. Lodge, Benfleet

Every Sunday evening at the Napoleon Inn at Boston in Lincolnshire, the ringing of a bell silenced the crowded bar. Then a voice called: 'Absent friends!' and glasses were raised to all those former customers serving in the armed forces. The weekly ceremony was connected to the pub's comfort fund that eventually raised over £1,000 for those absent friends.

David Smith, Lincoln

In 1945, Mrs K. Pearson of Southfield Avenue, Paignton, was expecting a parcel from her son, who was serving in the RAF. It contained his dirty laundry. A fortnight went by and still the parcel was not delivered. Then she received another letter from her son: 'Since I last wrote, my parcel has turned up, all nicely washed and ironed, with no word inside to show who had sent it.'

Letter to the *Sunday Express*, February 1945

LOOK,
DUCK AND
VANISH

I s that wonderful BBC television series *Dad's Army* in any way an accurate portrayal of Britain's Home Guard during the Second World War? After all, we would hardly think that another series, *'Allo 'Allo*, in any way reflects the French Resistance during those harrowing years. Yet one has the feeling that some of the goings-on in the Walmington-on-Sea platoon are not so far removed from reality.

It was on 14 May 1940 that an announcement was broadcast asking for volunteers for the Local Defence Volunteer Force. In August, the new prime minister, Winston Churchill, ordered the name to be changed to the Home Guard. What would become a legend in British history was born.

The original idea was that this citizens' army would try to delay invading German forces until the regular army could be rushed to the scene. But they were poorly armed and, as brave as they might have been, it is difficult to imagine them holding back a highly trained, well-armed force, using only a collection of sporting and museum-piece firearms and bread knives tied to broom handles. Eventually, better arms and better training transformed the original ragtag army into an organization that may well have proved an inconvenience to German paratroopers. But still . . .

The forming of the Home Guard was a response to what was already happening. As the threat of invasion became very real, up and down the country there were reports of bands of civilians arming themselves with shotguns, air rifles and pitchforks, ready to stick it to the Hun. The government had two options: to quash these grass-roots resistance fighters; or to harness them into an official organization. Thus, the Local Defence Volunteers were formed without any budget or any staff. And from there, as the Home Guard, it developed into something resembling a military force.

The early signs were encouraging, at least from the point of view of numbers if not of efficiency. Prime Minister Neville Chamberlain had told those interested to register their names at their local police station and they would be contacted when required. Inside the first twenty-four hours, more than a quarter of a million men had left their details, more than had been in Britain's regular peacetime army.

The government anticipated that around 150,000 men might answer the call to part-time arms. By the end of the second month, over one million had applied to join the LDV ('Look, Duck and Vanish', as it was unkindly dubbed in some quarters). By the time the Home Guard was stood down in December 1944 – the threat of invasion having long since passed – its number still stood at one million, and it had never dipped below that. A year later, on 31 December 1945, the organization was disbanded. But its name was indelibly printed on the history of the Second World War.

Nevertheless, the relationship between the Home Guard and

the War Office was generally an uneasy one. Lieutenant General Sir Henry Royds Pownall, the first Inspector General of the Local Defence Volunteer Force, complained: 'They are a troublesome and querulous lot . . . there is mighty little pleasing them, and the minority is always noisy.' (In the interests of balance, it should be noted that historian Brian D. Osborne, in his account of the Home Guard in Scotland, wrote that although Lieutenant General Pownall – who was Chief of General Staff for the British Expeditionary Force in France and Belgium until the fall of France in May 1940 – might have appeared 'a high-quality appointment', in fact, Field Marshal Montgomery thought him 'completely useless'.) All of which adds to our picture of how the Home Guard was viewed in some quarters.

My father-in-law joined the Home Guard in 1940. He was twenty-six years old and, as an engineer at the Rolls-Royce aero-engine factory, held a reserved occupation that prevented him from joining up – or saved him from that fate, whichever way one wants to look at it. Talking to him long after the war, I formed the opinion that the Home Guard platoon of which he was a member bore some resemblance to Captain Mainwaring's outfit. There seemed to be plenty of larks and zero danger. His recollection was that it was something akin to grown-up Boy Scouts. That is not to demean members of the Home Guard. If the Nazis had invaded the British mainland, even if their effectiveness would have been minimal, who is to say that the real Dad's Army wouldn't have fought bravely? In the meantime, they kept calm and carried on.

I was a supervisor at Luton Airport and joined the Home Guard. After being supplied with ill-fitting uniforms we had our first parade where the order was given that greatcoats must be worn. Unfortunately, I'd left mine in the car, so I rushed out to get it, put it on and then discovered that all the buttons had been cut off. My son had been swapping army buttons at school. Further along in the line, a colleague had buckled his belt inside out. The captain asked: 'Do you need to wear glasses?' But the worst of his scorn was reserved for the man next to me, who'd somehow managed to put on his greatcoat over his pack. The captain said: 'You should have been in the Camel Corps.'

When we had rifle practice, one man was firing away like mad at the target that was 200 yards away on a wall as big as a house. But not a mark was to be seen on the target. When the captain pointed this out, the man replied: 'Well, they're leaving here OK.'

Tom King, Flitwick, Bedfordshire

My husband was assigned to a Home Guard AA unit. It meant him rushing home from work and dashing to catch a train to the site. On the platform he came face-to-face with his CO and duly saluted smartly, only to be told that it was customary to salute an officer with the hat on the other way around.

Another incident that stays in my memory was the night my husband couldn't stop chuckling after he came off duty. It seems the squad were practising loading the anti-aircraft guns, and the ammunition was being passed from one man to another, and then to the man feeding the gun. The man in the middle of this operation had to walk several paces to hand over the ammunition. He took the ammo, walked a couple of paces, put it down carefully on the ground and fished in his pocket for his handkerchief, then blew his nose. The resulting bellow from the sergeant needs no description.

Zoe Paton, Southampton

The Home Guard was being drilled in a village near Plymouth.

'Number off!' said the sergeant.

One man started walking down the road.

'Hey, you!' said the sergeant. 'What do you think you're doing? Come back here!'

'Sorry, sir,' said the man. 'I thought you said bugger off!'

Mrs D. A. Hanning, Plymouth

This Home Guard private used to wear a wig under his cloth cap, but for night duty he was ordered to wear a metal helmet. Obviously it was nowhere near as comfortable as his cap, so at the first opportunity he discarded it. Someone found it and returned it to HQ. When he was asked how he'd lost it, he replied: 'It blew away in the wind, sir.'

An NCO who had a rather timid voice was drilling a company of Home Guard on the clifftop. When being marched towards a precipice, one of the front rank was heard to say: 'I wish he would say something – if only "Goodbye".'

A young Home Guard member was on the rifle range. Having overcome his fear of the weapon, he proceeded to place two hits on his own target and three on his neighbour's. Everyone fell about laughing when he received two reprimands – one for wasting ammunition, the other for spoiling someone else's target.

John Harvey, Launceston, Cornwall

I was working at A. V. Roe's Chadderton when I joined the Home Guard. About forty of us were on parade in a single line, with rifles and one round of live ammunition each, in an enclosed paddock by the side of the mill. At the far end of the line, the CO, a regular officer from a southern regiment, stood on a three-feet-high dais. All the lads on parade knew at least something about the firearm. I'd been on night work and, although I didn't know it, I'd missed quite an important part of the drill. The CO bawled the order to load. I hadn't a clue. I watched what was happening and followed suit, so I thought.

'Safety catches on!'

'Guv, where's the safety catch?'

'Fire your rifle!'

'Hell's bells,' I said to the bloke on my right, 'where's the safety catch?'

He gave me a startled look, but offered no help.

'Fire your rifles!'

In a cold sweat I squeezed the trigger . . . whee-ee-ee! The bullet flew out, high into the heavens. Every eye was on me.

'Step out that man!'

I stepped one pace forward.

'Why wasn't the safety catch on? Sergeant, this man must have rifle drill. He's shot an old woman in Urmston.'

Fred Cawte, Heywood, Lancashire

During the very early days of the war, we lived in a row of houses that faced the local electricity supply company and power station. We had long back gardens with side entrances that led out onto the road just opposite. One Sunday morning we were startled to see a whole row of camouflaged men creeping up through the back gardens. My seventy-year-old aunt, whose word was law in the house, threw open the bedroom window and called down to ask who they were and what, precisely, they were doing. The sergeant quickly stood up and said that they were the local Home Guard on a practice manoeuvre. They were, it seemed, pretending to 'storm' the electric company. But Auntie said:

'Never mind that, you must all clear off at once.'

'Sorry, ma'am, but there is a war on and we must practise. What would you say if we were Germans?' the sergeant asked.

'The same as I am telling you lot! I never allow anyone to trample all over my garden.'

Mrs M. Wilkinson, Uxbridge

My young brother was in the Home Guard, prior to joining the RAF. He was sent out one night to help search for a German airman, alleged to have parachuted into the area.

My brother found himself in the pitch dark, beside a high fence, from the other side of which he could hear an agitated shuffling. He scrambled up to look over but slid down the other side and into the middle of a flock of hens!

Getting to his feet, he stumbled about as he tried to get out of the garden, stepping on a rake, the handle of which sprang up and hit the rim of his helmet with a loud clang. He remarked that, after all that racket, any German would have made for Land's End.

Miss P. Manser, Maidstone

My husband was Grade 4 so did not join up but went into the Home Guard. One night he was on duty at Battersea Power Station by the Thames. Suddenly he saw a lot of white objects floating along the river. It being very dark, owing to the blackout, he mistook these mystery objects for German parachutes. Only when they got nearer did he realize they were a family of swans!

Lucy Glasby (née Harris),
Clapham Junction

My father, 'Jack the Barber' (a hairdresser), and his friend 'Fishy' (who kept the local chip shop) were First World War veterans. One night, during the Second World War, they came out of the local pub in Jarrow. They staggered home, both a little the worse for wear. Just as they passed the nearby barrage balloon site, manned by the Home Guard, a voice boomed out: 'Halt, who goes there? Stop, or I'll shoot!'

The reply from the two merry men?

'Bugger off, Jim, or we'll stop your fish and chips!'

And, with added disdain: 'Anyway, you've not got a bloody gun! It's only a bloody stick!'

Mr G. W. Telford, Northampton

As an RAF pilot, I was flying a Miles Magister over Allestree Park in Derby. Our brief was to give the Home Guard a chance to guess at what height we were flying and let them have a bit of aiming practice as well. Only when we got back to base did we realize they were using live ammunition. One bullet had gone straight between my knees. The young officer in charge told an inquiry: 'We thought they were armour-plated. In any case, we never thought we'd hit them!'

George Watson, Derby

I was in one of the Home Guard platoons attached to the Rolls-Royce aero-engine factory in Derby where I worked. We always expected to be a target for the Luftwaffe because the Merlin engines were manufactured there. But there was only ever one successful raid and that was in 1942 when a lone Dornier got through and bombed and machine-gunned the factory. Several people were killed, sadly, but production wasn't really affected. Anyway, we were always on the alert but one weekend we were taken to a camp near Skegness to practise on the anti-aircraft guns.

To be honest, we looked upon it as a bit of a break beside the seaside and, by and large, that is how it turned out. Our accommodation block was very basic, though, and the lavatories were quite a long walk away, so in the middle of the night, one by one, when nature called we relieved ourselves in a farmer's field across the road.

On the following lunchtime, we were called in for our midday meal and served some meat and veg. One of the lads remarked how nice the cabbage was, whereupon one of the cooks said: 'Yes, freshly picked a couple of hours ago.' We asked from where and he waved his hand and said: 'Out of that field opposite.' It was the one we'd been using as a lavatory all night. Suddenly the cabbage didn't seem as tasty and he couldn't understand why, after complimenting him on it, everyone instead started leaving it on their plates.

Bernard Buckler, Derby

I was in the Home Guard in Lincolnshire and it was one of those brilliant, moonlit nights when it seemed as though everywhere was bathed in a bright light. We heard a lone aircraft overhead but, despite the clear night, couldn't actually see it. Eventually, the noise of its engines receded and once more there was silence. Then someone pointed to a tree in the distance. There was a white parachute in it. We debated whether to tackle the German invader ourselves, but in the end decided to call out the regular army lads from the nearby camp. Were our faces red! The parachute turned out to be nothing more than a thick covering of white spring blossom. We all had a good laugh, though.

Geoff Hemmings, London

In 1940, I joined what was still the Local Defence Volunteers in Cheltenham. My occupation as a plumber and slater, plus my age group – I was then thirty-one – put me in the deferred call-up class for military service. I owned a motorcycle so I became the despatch rider. I was also very keen to improve on anything that I considered to be out-of-date thinking.

One sunny Sunday morning, seventy-two of us went to the local shooting butts to fire six rounds each at targets 2,500 yards away. We arrived about 9.30 a.m. and left about 7 p.m. But about sixty per cent of that time was taken up using flags to signal back target hits. Now I'd been building radios since I was eleven, so when we returned to the range three weeks later, I produced a simple device with a 'speak/listen' switch together with loudspeakers. It was a great success and reduced by more than half the time we spent on the range. We were getting the 'target hit' signal straight away rather than waiting for the flags. The only thing was that it cost £4 10s [£4.50], which I had to pay.

We also had to guard a length of railway line from nightfall to daybreak, with instructions that if a German paratrooper dropped in, we had to disarm him, tie his hands behind his back and walk him to HQ, leaving some of our men to stay on guard. It seemed to me that we needed to inform HQ immediately, but that drum beating was a little 'old hat' while smoke signals would work only in daytime. So I constructed another radio transmitter, one that could have us reporting any incident to HQ within seconds.

I combed numerous radio shops and second-hand dealers, and put an advertisement in the local newspaper, and eventually I had sufficient parts to build my radio. Five weeks later I had all I needed, including an alarm clock for transmitting a 'tick-tock' to test it. It worked like a dream and so I decided to show it to our local MP, Daniel Lipson. I took only the receiver to his house and assured him that we wouldn't be breaking the law as there was nothing illegal about receiving radio signals, only sending them. When he heard the 'tick-tock' being transmitted from my home, he was taken aback and told me to put the whole thing out of sight and that he'd contact me in due course. Well, when his answer came it was: 'No can do.'

I knew what would happen next, so I put the apparatus away, together with a postcard that read: 'Made by J.M.S. for use by HG – maybe. Date completed and checked 1 October 1940. Cost of construction (pair) £14 10s 0d.' Then I waited.

Seventy-two hours later there was a knock on our front door. There stood two detectives. They had it on good authority that I had in my possession instruments for the transmission of radio signals contrary to Section 8 of the Defence of the Realm Act. I was taken to the police station where my story was taken down and I was put in a cell, together with a deserter who was waiting for the Military Police. I thought: 'Isn't it marvellous? He's in here for shirking his duty and I'm in here for overdoing mine.'

Finally, in the early evening, they took me back upstairs. Some technical bods had examined my radio and I was free to go. It was smiles all round. They even laid on a car. My first stop was home to pick up my Home Guard kit. My second stop was the Home Guard HQ, where I handed in my resignation. I was fed up of playing at soldiers.

The following day, my old CO asked me if I'd go with him to see the officer commanding the Home Guard in the area. The OC thanked me for my efforts in trying to improve communications and make my unit one of the most up-to-date. He said that my radio was being sent to Southern Command for testing, but later I was told that it had been impounded 'for the duration of the war'.

Just after that Christmas I received my call-up papers. I passed my medical and then was interviewed by a selection officer. I noticed that my card had one difference to everyone else's: there was a dotted red line under my name. I wondered if it was some sort of code, some hint about my tangle with the authorities over my radio apparatus. Anyway, the selection officer said that he thought it unlikely that I would be called up – and I never was! I still think I was right, though, in doing what I did.

J. M. Seward, Seaton, Devon

We were going on patrol one night and our officer, a rather toffee-nosed chap who had fought in the First World War, got us together and gave us what he thought was a pep talk. His final words were: 'Remember chaps, if the invasion comes tonight, then we must not let the enemy past.' And one little private piped up from the back: 'No chance of that, sir. They'll never catch us!'

Ivor Townsend, Redditch

We had this officer in charge of our Home Guard unit in Norfolk. He was a real old duffer from the First World War. The rumour was that he'd never seen active service then, just served in office jobs in England. I don't know if that was true because he sported a chest full of medal ribbons. I can't imagine that he'd have been awarded so many if he'd never left our shores. Nevertheless, we resented him because he never stopped showing off, constantly reminding us about his previous war service. One day he turned up on parade with even more medal ribbons. There was hardly any room left. He was inspecting us and as he walked past, from the middle of our ranks came a voice: 'Blimey, he's got a note on there saying, "Continued on the back."

The officer spun round and said: 'Who said that?'

No one owned up and it took us all our time to control our laughter.

There was another bloke in our platoon who was on patrol, walking down a country road, when a car came round the corner. The lad jumped into the middle of the road and shouted: 'Halt!' So the driver stopped and the lad said again: 'Halt!'

The driver said: 'I've halted. What more do you want me to do?'

And the lad replied: 'I don't know. My orders are to say "Halt" three times – and then shoot.'

Sometimes, it really was difficult to take the war all that seriously down in deepest Norfolk.

Dennis Roberts, Reading

Our Home Guard unit contained a couple of locals who were well-known poachers. I don't know how they got hold of spare ammunition but they never returned from night patrol without a couple of dead rabbits under their coats. One was a real dead loss, to be honest, and there was this famous occasion when he was on sentry duty, on his own, and the officer decided to test him out. When he heard footsteps in the dark, instead of the regulation 'Halt, who goes there?', he called out: 'Is that you, Harold?' Harold was his mate, the other poacher. It was all very laid-back stuff. Bit of fun and games, really, I suppose.

Roy Burns, Dorset

We had to stage an attack on a rival Home Guard platoon who were supposed to be defending a water tower. I think we took it a lot more seriously then they did, though, because we were creeping up on them in the dark when suddenly there was a hell of a commotion – voices and then the sound of footsteps hurrying – and then complete silence. We wondered what trick they were playing and we lay there for about a quarter of an hour before gingerly making our way forward again. When we got within range of the water tower, we still couldn't see anybody. The place was deserted. The other lot had apparently decided to unilaterally call the exercise to a halt because they realized that it was opening time and there was a pub down the road. It was probably a good job that the Germans never landed.

Bernard Buckler, Derby

Early one morning, I was on duty with a few others and we were looking for a German pilot who had come down the afternoon before. One of the lads shouted out that they had found him hiding up Conyer Creek.

It was about a hundred yards away so we all ran over to the hiding spot. It was very marshy over there and there was lots of swearing as one or another fell over.

When we got there a farmer with a pitch fork was standing over a very frightened German pilot who was sitting with his hands in the air. He must have had a very cold night and he looked pretty pleased to be captured.

We took him away, but the farmer made sure he was in the lead with his pitchfork right up behind him. The pilot was more scared of the farmer than he was us and our old rifles.

Norman Luckhurst, Kent

In 1940 I was eighteen, and my pal, Arthur, seventeen. Only those who experienced those nervous days, after the fall of France, can appreciate the fervour of patriotism that gripped the country and caused Arthur and myself, among a million others, young and not so young, to sign up for what was then called the Local Defence Volunteers.

To begin with, we were put through the complications of arms drill by 'old sweats', who showed much restraint each time rifles evaded stiff fingers and clattered to the ground. One of the ways to stop a tank, we were told, was to place an upturned dinner plate on the road. The tank driver, mistaking this for an anti-tank mine, would probably bring his tank to a halt. The rest was easy: wait for the tank hatch to open, then lob in a grenade. It sounded all right and the younger ones especially seemed to be taking it in. But I had a little nagging doubt myself. If this neat trick had already been tried out in France, then it couldn't have worked all that well.

Anyway, after a fortifying drink or two had helped us ready ourselves to take on the whole Nazi army if necessary, Arthur and me set off around 9.30 on a Friday evening to report for our first night guard duty. Searching for our headquarters, a deserted farmhouse, we had just crossed a boggy field when all at once a voice came from out of the darkness.

'Stop!' it said. Then, 'Halt! I mean: Halt! Who goes there?'

'Us,' said Arthur. There was a bit of a pause.

'You can't say that,' went the voice, sort of indignant. 'You gotta say it. You gotta say "Friend or foe".'

'Friend or foe,' obliged Arthur.

After a longer pause, I could just make out this shadowy figure approaching us, holding what looked like a broom handle with a bayonet tied to it. 'You gotta be one thing or the other,' it complained, getting nearer. 'I mean, I'm supposed to make you say it.' By then the sharp end of the bayonet was waving close to our faces. 'You gotta say it.'

'We're LDV,' I answered before Arthur could further complicate our arrival.

At the broomstick end of the weapon, the shadow took on a tin-hatted, white disc of a face wearing glasses. 'How do I know you're not just saying that? For all I know you could be foe.'

'We ain't got bloody parachutes on. We got armbands on, see!' said Arthur, now getting a tad aggressive, thanks to the beer. 'Ain't you got no torch?'

The bayonet lowered itself. 'We're still waiting for new batteries, like. Hold on, though, I've got some matches here. I'd better make sure, hadn't I?'

After some scraping, a flaring match broke through the blackout while this fearless guard scrutinized our armbands. We could then see he was a long-faced youth with two prominent teeth. 'Yeah, that's right, you got armbands on,' he conceded. 'Bit late, ain't you?'

'We'll be a bloody sight later before you've done,' complained Arthur.

What a pantomime!

Harold Richardson, Derby

139

MAKE DO
AND MEND

In 1944, Archibald Brown of Tower Hill, Bruton, in Somerset, was fined £4 plus £6 costs for wasting butter, margarine, cheese, lard, bread, bacon, pickles and preserved plums. His crime? He threw them at his wife. The solicitor representing the Ministry of Food told the court at Wincanton: 'If there is any acrimonious debate in the home or any breach of connubial bliss, rations must not be used as weapons of war.'

Archibald Brown obviously didn't keep calm and carry on. And neither did John Jackson, a miner from Low Valley, near Barnsley, who was sent to prison for one month after throwing eggs and bacon on the fire and sugar and tea on the floor after his wife refused to lend him five shillings (25p). The chairman of the magistrates said: 'Wasting food in wartime will not be tolerated.'

Each case summed up one of the great issues of the Second World War: the shortage of food, the rationing of which gave rise to plenty of examples of how the people of Britain set about to 'make do and mend'. There must have been thousands of Second World War wedding cakes that comprised no more than an iced cardboard shell.

Of course, food wasn't the only commodity to be rationed. From September 1939, petrol was available only for business or essential purposes. Furniture became utilitarian. Clothing too: pleats and turn-ups disappeared from trousers, and garments were mostly plain. Women painted gravy browning on bare legs as a replacement for silk stockings, then recruited the services of a small child to draw a 'seam' using an eyebrow pencil. Eventually, when eyebrow pencils themselves were in short supply, a spent match had to suffice.

But it was food shortages that dominated the nation's thoughts. And Archibald Brown and John Jackson weren't the only Britons to be fined for wasting it. In January 1943, for instance, a Hertfordshire woman was fined £10 with £2 costs for 'permitting bread to be wasted'. The court in Barnet heard that her servant – who was also fined five shillings (25p) – was twice seen throwing bread to birds in her employer's garden. 'Miss XYZ', as she was identified, admitted that she put bread out every day. 'I cannot see the birds starve,' she told the court.

Indeed, there were many unusual legal battles surrounding wartime food regulations. A man appeared at Tavistock Petty Sessions charged with selling eggs to unregistered customers. It was alleged that he kept twenty-five hens and four cocks when the law stated that only twenty-five head of poultry was allowed. The Ministry of Food claimed that this counted as 'poultry' according to the Oxford English Dictionary, but magistrates threw out the case, declaring that only laying hens counted.

Food rationing began in January 1940, with bacon, ham, butter and sugar the first to be restricted. It wasn't long before meat, tea, cooking fat and cheese were also rationed, and by 1942 almost everything else was too. Imagine: a grown adult was allowed only one fresh egg per week. Unless they were pregnant, of course, then they could have two.

The Ministry of Food, under Lord Woolton, was responsible for overseeing rationing. Every man, woman and child was given a ration book with coupons that had to be produced before rationed goods could be purchased. Housewives had to register with particular retailers, which lessened the need to queue (as people did in the First World War when rationing wasn't introduced until 1918) but as shortages increased, so long queues for unrationed goods became commonplace. Word would spread: 'Mr Brown has had a delivery of onions.' And housewives would rush to his shop. Sometimes, though, they joined queues without actually knowing what reward would be at the end of it. There are few reports of disturbances. When it came to food rationing, people seemed to have kept very calm.

They also carried on. The Ministry of Food's 'Dig For Victory' campaign encouraged self-sufficiency, and the number of allotments rose from 815,000 to 1.4 million. The BBC's *Radio Allotment* grew twenty-three kinds of vegetable, with weekly wireless reports on progress. Pigs, chickens and rabbits were reared domestically for meat; vegetables were grown anywhere that could be cultivated. By 1940, as we have seen, wasting food was a criminal offence, whether you were feeding bread to the birds or aiming jars of pickles at your wife.

Meanwhile, the Second World War lifted the status of the humble carrot to an almost mystical level. It became the food that Britons believed could win the war. Curried carrot, carrot jam, carrot pudding, and a homemade drink called 'Carrolade' – they were new culinary delights to lift the spirit of a war-weary nation.

Most of all, though, it was the carrot that apparently won the air battle against the Luftwaffe. Therefore, so far as civilians were concerned, it was the veg that could help you 'see in the dark', which was quite useful in blacked-out Britain.

It started when the government responded to an oversupply of carrots by hinting that the RAF's exceptional success in night-flying operations was due to pilots being fed high-carotene-content carrots. Even Walt Disney lent a hand, creating a carrot family that included Carroty George, Clara Carrot, and Dr Carrot, for British newspapers to promote the eating of carrots.

The propaganda worked. The nation flocked to buy or grow carrots. Whether the Nazis also bought the notion, or whether they rightly assumed that the RAF's success was due more to the increased sophistication of radar, is not clear. It didn't matter. The problem of too many carrots was being solved.

Besides its *Radio Allotment*, the BBC also broadcast a daily five-minute programme, *The Kitchen Front*, that advised on new food sources and creative recipes – not all of them sounded too appealing.

And then there was the 'Black Market' which actually prospered further when peace was declared because, in the early post-war years, food rationing became more severe. My mother had already made a huge compromise with her morals. Despite being scrupulously honest almost to the point of eccentricity, after war was declared, the Black Market was one area where she soon became happy to dabble on the wrong side of the law. Down our street lived a busy little woman who I knew only as Mrs Potter. She could often be seen scurrying about the neighbourhood after dark, lugging a huge sack on her back. One winter's evening, I answered the door to her furtive knock, to be told in an anxious whisper: 'Go and see if your mother wants any tea.' Naturally my mother did want some tea – or sugar, or butter, or anything else that was on ration – and money and consumables changed hands on the darkened front step. The goods had been stolen, of course, but even otherwise law-abiding housewives desperately wanted to put a little extra on their families' tables. Keeping calm and carrying on, you see.

Actually, it was all too easy to break the law. A soldier posted to the Isle of Man took the advice of Lord Woolton and saved up his sugar ration for jam-making. When he was posted back to the mainland, he found that he could not take the sugar with him. In fact a law blocked his every alternative. He could not take it with him because the Ministry of Food refused him a permit. He could not sell it because he had no licence to trade in sugar. He could not destroy it because that was against food regulations. He could not give it away because it was illegal to allow another person to obtain sugar from his ration coupons. A Manx government official stated: 'We cannot allow all and sundry to take sugar away from the Isle of Man.' What eventually happened to the soldier's sugar hoard is not recorded.

People were desperate for certain items and a lot of bartering went on. One newspaper advertisement read: 'Swap peach bedlinen for nylon stockings or honey Victorian cheese dish for 1 dozen new handkerchiefs.' Another said: 'Set of frying pans for suit for 1 public schoolboy.'

Some food items became a national joke. In December 1944, solicitors acting for the American company that marketed Spam, the canned pre-cooked meat product first introduced in 1937, complained that a joke by Sonnie Hale in the pantomime *Aladdin* at Manchester Hippodrome, referring to the smell of burning Spam, implied that Spam was not a suitable food. The Americans obviously thought jokes about Spam had gone too far.

Then there were pets to think about. At a Home Guard post near the Admiralty, the men adopted a large black cat. It was put 'on the strength' and drew a daily allowance of half a pint of milk. Then it was discovered that the cat was already drawing rations from the Royal Navy. The matter was brought to the attention of the Admiralty, and the cat was withdrawn from Home Guard rations

Of course, if food was in short supply, cosmetics most certainly were. Yet women were still encouraged to maintain a groomed look, even though this took a fair degree of ingenuity. In 1940, a book entitled *Technique For Beauty* told women: 'The stress and strain of war can easily make you lose interest in your personal appearance. But it is up to you to take care of yourself for the sake of other people.' There were also practical considerations. For instance, Pond's Cold Cream was promoted as a way to prevent women working outdoors from developing ruddy complexions and chapped lips.

There was also something called 'day lotion' produced by Cyclax, one of the oldest cosmetic companies in Britain. The lotion came in wartime shade choices with bewildering names such as Peach, Light Rachel, Rachel, Deep Rachel, Dark Rachel, Sunburn No 1 and Sunburn No 2. Cyclax also produced a burns cream and a camouflage cream, and the company also suffered badly in the Blitz when its factory on Tottenham Court Road was destroyed by enemy action. Surely Hermann Goering wasn't targeting the cosmetics industry in a bid to ruin British morale?

I was a shy, freckled child of five or six and an only child at the time. My father was away in the army, so it was just my mother and I.

I was sent on an errand to a distant shop for a tin of Spam. It seems like it's miles away when you've only got little five-year-old legs! The old dragon who kept the shop snapped from behind the counter: 'We have no Spam. Take this home instead!' So I ran home with the precious tin of meat. My mother was less impressed. She yelled at me: 'What's this – snoek*? I don't want blinking snoek. Take it back! What's she trying to get rid of this for on you?' I went back into the shop trembling and waiting to be executed by the dragon, who calmly refunded my money instead.

Brenda Shaw, Hull

*'Snoek' was popularly claimed to be 'whale meat' but was in fact a fish mostly from South African waters. It was just unfamiliar to the British who began to treat it as a national joke.

I remember reading that a lemon sent home from the Middle East by a Chertsey soldier raised more than £6 when it was raffled in aid of Red Cross funds. A Mrs Lemon won it. That made everyone chuckle.

BRIAN ORMSBY, LONDON

I'm relating a story, which my husband always told as if it had happened to us, but it actually happened to a friend of his. Here is the story:

We received a food parcel from our cousins in Melbourne, Australia. It contained enough dried fruits to make both a Christmas cake and a Christmas pudding. Plus a small unlabelled packet, which I assumed to be spice.

I made the puddings and cake. Then we received a letter, which we should have received before the fruit parcel arrived. It told us that the fruit was on its way and that a very special package was to be included. A small packet containing the ashes of a dear friend whose dying wish had been to have his ashes scattered from the Clifton Suspension Bridge. There was only one thing for it: the cake and the pudding had to be scattered from the bridge!

Mrs G. Horner, Bristol

During the rationing of food, one was always on the lookout for queues to secure anything that was going. A woman asked a man at the end of a queue what the line was for and he told her: '*Tales of Hoffman.*'

After a moment's hesitation, she murmured, half to herself: 'Well I suppose they could always make some soup!'

James Walker, Aberdeen

When I was driving for the WVS, I served a variety of passengers, including Lord Keynes, the economist, and various civil servants, often from the Ministry of Information. Two particular ladies, from the Ministry of Food, always instructed me 'to bring nosebags' and we used to sit outside factories munching sandwiches. Usually my passengers would fix a meal where we were going, or sometimes we'd go for a 'five bob's worth' at one of the British Restaurants that were run by local authorities and subsidized to provide nutritious food for people.

Leila Mackinlay, London

For seven years I had known the tranquillity of country life when my peace was shattered by the news that Hitler had entered Poland and we had declared war on Germany. I knew I had to do something towards the war effort. I could have become a 'Land Girl', but my decision to join the NAAFI was encouraged by a friend of mine who was already a member of the service. With forms filled in and a medical report that said I was A1, I packed my cardboard suitcase and made for my first assignment, which was a barracks where thousands of troops waited for transport to go overseas.

From a quiet existence I was plunged into noise and people, and for a while I found it hard to accept, but eventually became accustomed to it, and part of it. I was to bake cakes for hungry boys and, under the supervision of another girl, learned the tricks of the baking trade. I made thousands of rock cakes that lived up to their names when they cooled off, thanks to the lack of fat in the recipe.

It was surprising what one pound of flour, two ounces of margarine and a few currants could make. Sausage rolls were eaten by the dozen, and a concoction called 'Nelson' was a great favourite. This had a pastry base with a bread-pudding filling and a pastry topping. It smelled very good and spicy when it was baked but weighed a ton when lifted from the oven. It certainly kept the soldiers on the ground after they had tasted it!

However, it was all devoured enthusiastically by the troops, but I was often teased about whose side I was on! One declared I was 'Hitler's secret weapon' trying to kill them off!

Gwyneth Wright, London

If news got around that a certain shop had a certain rare commodity, there would be a 'stampede' and queues a mile long. I remember stampedes for potato crisps (only one packet per family) and bananas (one per person). The cry would go up: 'Brown's have got some custard creams!' and whoosh, a queue of kids had formed in seconds.

Brenda Shaw, Hull

At Christmastime most people took their mixed cake – made from fruit and other ingredients that had been hoarded for months – to the baker's along the road for cooking. Nanny lived with Granddad in one house, and her two married daughters lived one house away. So, when the girls arrived home to find the cakes had been mixed, they wanted to know what she had done about lemon essence, as this was in their pantry. Nanny said she'd got some in her own pantry, but it turned out to be yellow Brilliantine [a hair product] left there by one of the sons! We'd spent so long collecting all the ingredients that we daren't waste them, so had the cakes baked anyway.

Mrs B. M. Hipperson

One of the most notable things about the war was the shortage of cigarettes. When you could get them, all sorts of unfamiliar names began to appear on packets. One day, a lady waiting in a queue with my mother said: 'I'm dying for a fag. Can you see any?'

Regular customers of the shop knew that 'special' items were often put aside under the counter or to one side, so my mother leaned over to have a look before spotting yet another unfamiliar brand of cigarettes.

'They've got some packets of "Push"', she answered proudly, not realizing that, in those days before flip-top packs, she was simply reading the opening instructions on the side of the packet.

Mrs E. Cross, Bexley, Kent

One recalls the wedding of one of the girls on 'B' shift to a young soldier who had been working in another part of the building and then been diverted to REME. Our staff were not supposed to mingle, but love had triumphed and the courtship was largely conducted by him ringing the message room from a phone box at the corner and having a chat to his Mavis when no alert was on. We managed to provide, between us, the necessary ingredients to give her a proper wedding cake. We were all very fond of the Tchaikovsky concerto, which formed one of the records in our gramophone club. Unbeknown to the bride and groom, we arranged for the organist to play this piece when they were about to go and sign the register. Who could forget the incredible joy on Mavis' face as she halted and stood still until it was finished?

Leila Mackinlay, London

I know we had to be inventive when it came to doing our best with whatever food was available. But when I think of some of the things we concocted – fish in savoury custard, mock crab made from dried egg, margarine and cheese, dripping cake – it makes me wonder how we survived the war.

Beryl Bentley, Derby

I was working in a newsagent's during the war but have some notes of letters received at the Milk Office, asking for free milk.

'Please send me a form for cheap milk, as I'm expecting mother.'

'Please send me a form for cheap milk for having children at reduced prices.'

'Please send me a form for free milk. I posted the form by mistake before my child was filled in properly.'

'I have a baby 18 months old, thanking you for same.'

'Please send me a form, I have a baby two months old and didn't know anything about it until a friend told me.'

'I have a baby fed entirely on cows and another four months old.'

'I have been in bed two weeks with my baby and didn't know it was running out until my milkman told me.'

Betty Quigley, Glasgow

My grandmother was quite a character. She was largely uneducated and caused uproar on many occasions. Her three sons were called up to fight and, because her husband was poorly, she worried about how she would manage financially without her boys' help. An official called at her house, to reassure Nanny that she would be granted an allotment. Apparently, this bothered her all morning until the rest of the family arrived back shortly after midday. She wailed to them that an allotment would be no use to Granddad, since he had never done any digging in his life!

Mrs B. M. Hipperson

My father, sisters and nephew lived in Hartshorne in Derbyshire. My sister and I took a bus to Burton upon Trent to buy my nephew a pair of new shoes. In one of the big shops, we selected a pair and then enquired about the price. The assistant told us the cost, which 'includes the tax'. I was astonished. 'Do you mean that we have to nail them together ourselves?'

My sister, crossing her legs tightly and stifling a snigger, had to explain to me that the assistant was talking about the purchase tax, which had recently been applied to many items. I felt, and looked, such a fool.

Mrs Z. Price, Withington

Nanny had many upsets with shopping, although never with reckoning money. She would know exactly what was what in that department. But at the butcher's shop, suet was in short supply and allocated according to surname initials. Nanny was unaware of this and, on seeing suet, she asked for some, only to be told that she had her allowance 'with the Ps'. She came home totally bemused, complaining to the family that poor Mr Orford was obviously going mad because he didn't even sell peas.

Mrs B. M. Hipperson

My aunt had two seven-year-old evacuees from London billeted on her just a few weeks after war broke out. Having arrived on the Saturday night, they all sat down to Sunday dinner of roast beef, potatoes, carrots and kidney beans. One of the boys just sat and looked at his plate. My aunt asked him what was wrong and with that the boy scooped up the kidney beans and threw them on the fire saying in his strong cockney accent: 'I don't eat bloody grass in London and I'm not eating it here!'

My aunt asked him what he usually had for dinner at home. He replied: 'Brown beer and doughnuts!'

Mrs P. Pitman, Clevedon, Avon

Women might have been in the services but they were still encouraged to wear a bit of make-up. In fact, a pamphlet was issued. It pointed out that while long varnished fingernails wasn't conducive to service life, varnish bases would help us prevent cracked nails. I think the Wrens were actually issued with a red lipstick that, it was thought, would complement their uniforms. And, of course, it was itself uniform.

I think that the best tip, though, was not to paint your eyelashes if you were likely to be putting on a service respirator. After you'd been wearing one of those for a few minutes, it had a tendency to steam up with condensation from your breath, which, of course, would make cosmetics run into your eyes.

Beryl Hockey, London

Just as the war was coming to an end, I was scheduled to go to Leeds as a bus conductress with the long-distance buses. It was a bitter January day and it started to snow. To get to Leeds we had to travel over some bleak moors. By the time we reached Leeds, the snow was falling thick and fast with flakes that seemed almost as big as the palm of my hand. I went to the toilet and could hear a strange gurgling sound coming from the next cubicle. I thought someone was being taken ill so I called out to ask whether they were all right.

There was no answer, but the gurgling continued, so I went to the station inspector who used his master key to open the cubicle door. Inside stood a naked woman, washing her clothes in the toilet bowl. She claimed that, despite it being the coldest day of the winter so far, she would put on her wet clothes and the warmth of her body would dry them.

Mrs Z. Price, Withington

Grandma Buggins on *The Kitchen Front* remarked this morning: 'Well, if you don't care about the nice recipes I bring you, I might as well go to Russia and fish for surgeons in the vodka.'

EXTRACT FROM THE DIARY OF MISS C. M. EDWARDS,
LINCOLNSHIRE, JANUARY 1942

One of the worst shortages – well, for a woman at least – was elastic. Particularly knicker elastic. Imagine that you were walking down the street and suddenly you realized that your knickers were falling down! You had a couple of options: you could bend down and take them from around your ankles and put them in your handbag, which was humiliating; or you could step out of them and walk on as though nothing had happened. But then you would lose a perfectly good pair of knickers. Actually, there was a third option – if you had enough warning. When you felt them going, you might be able to grab them from outside your dress, and then do a funny walk until you found somewhere private where you could sort them out. That happened to me once when a boy was taking me to the pictures. I managed to get into the ladies' toilet, but I think he'd already spotted that something was wrong from the way I was walking, all bandy-legged all of a sudden. Still, it was wartime. We had to carry on.

Edith Smith, London

In May 1941, the *Daily Express* reported that, determined to overcome the shortage of eggs, two resourceful climbers descended the 400-feet cliffs at Bempton on the Yorkshire coast and collected 350 seabird eggs that they said they hoped to sell for 2-3 shillings (10-15p) a dozen. The newspaper did not say whether their venture was successful, or indeed legal.

The authorities came down very hard on petrol rationing. I remember that there was a court case where a man from Derby was fined for wasting petrol because he was caught driving to watch Derby County. But another chap got round this by taking his mates to the football in a furniture van. They all crowded inside around a piano. His plan was that, if the police stopped him, he would say that his journey was essential because he was delivering the piano to the NAAFI. He never was stopped and drove that piano back and forth, from his house to the football ground, for about two years.

Bernard Buckler, Derby

It was a funny thing travelling in the war because you weren't allowed petrol and couldn't have coaches. We had a chap on the committee whose job involved moving furniture about. He brought this wagon one day when we were playing at Chester. There were no seats or anything. We all got in with our bags and were dropped in an isolated part of Chester and then walked in as though we'd come on the train.

Harold Bell, Tranmere Rovers player

Sport, in particular football, played a vital role in maintaining the nation's morale, and although the official competitions were suspended upon the outbreak of war, regional leagues were soon organized using 'guest players', mostly pre-war footballers now in the armed forces and allowed to play for clubs near to where they were stationed. This 'make-do-and-mend' football produced some bizarre incidents.

You never knew which team was which because blokes were coming home on leave and then couldn't get [to the match] . . . I've been at Goodison and it's come over the tannoy: 'Any footballers in the crowd?' Some fans used to go to the game with their boots, just in case . . .

Harold Atkinson, Tranmere Rovers

I lost count of the number of clubs I played for during the war. Many clubs used so many guests that they were hardly recognizable. Once I played for six different league clubs in little more than a week. After I was posted to a camp at Skegness, for instance, I played for Lincoln City and Grimsby Town, switching between the two quite regularly. I can't imagine how the fans felt. Some weeks there were so many changes that it was hardly worth printing the team sheets. But it was a game of football.

Peter Doherty, Poulton-le-Fylde

I was working at an electrical factory and playing amateur football when the war started. In 1940–41, at the age of seventeen, I found myself in Leicester City's first team, playing inside right to a little right winger called Billy Wright, whose own club, Wolverhampton Wanderers, had closed down for that season. I had no idea that my right-wing partner would one day win a record number of England caps from the half-back line. A lot of the Leicester players had joined up and that gave opportunities to youngsters like me. I made my debut in May 1940, against Wolves, and managed to score twice, but my best memory was playing against Stanley Matthews in a snowstorm at Stoke. It was beyond my wildest dreams to play against someone like him and I had the war to thank for it. I was just a baby really. The biggest problem was getting time off to play.

Jack Smith, Leicester

Make-do-and-mend football certainly threw up some strange incidents. On Christmas Day 1941, Bristol City set off in three cars to play Southampton at The Dell. By kick-off time, only the car carrying the kit and two players had arrived. The match eventually kicked off one hour late, with the Bristol team completed by five Southampton reserves, the Saints' trainer, and three spectators. Twenty minutes into the game, the missing Bristol players arrived, crammed into one car. The other vehicle had broken down en route. At half-time, Southampton were winning 3–0 and one of the spectators in the Bristol team decided that he could not carry on. City decided to slip on one of the late arrivals, Ernie Brinton, who changed into the dirty kit and rubbed mud on his knees before trotting out for the second half. Within seconds of the restart, a linesman spotted the ringer and Brinton had to leave the field. In the circumstances it was surprising that Southampton won by only 5–2.

Sometimes the manager himself had to turn out to make up the numbers. On 20 January 1940, Swindon Town found themselves with only ten men at the Aero Engines Company Ground at Kingswood for their match against Bristol City. Swindon's manager, Neil Harris, forty-three years old, his previous competitive match over nine years earlier, was forced to turn out in borrowed boots too small for him. Swindon lost 5–2 and Harris lost two toenails.

A young man turned up at Chelsea claiming to be a well-known Motherwell player. The manager, Billy Birrell, had only ten men and even though the stranger looked an unlikely footballer, Birrell had little option but to play him. After only a few minutes, Birrell's worst fears were confirmed. The crowd were also quick to spot that the new man had hardly played the game. All Birrell could do was leave him on the pitch and tell the rest of the Chelsea team not to pass the ball to him.

Northampton Town's use of guest players – in 1941-2 alone, two-thirds of their players came from the ranks of other clubs – produced an interesting character. In January 1944, they gave a chance to a young man called Hess, of all names, who claimed to have played for one of Austria's leading clubs before the war. He turned out on the right wing in a 3-0 defeat at Walsall. He was quite awful but Northampton were stuck with him for the whole ninety minutes. Then they said their farewells and Herr Hess disappeared from Northampton Town's history even quicker than he had entered it.

In October 1943, the Charlton manager, Jimmy Seed, had to apologise to supporters: 'I feel that it is somewhat necessary for me to attempt some sort of apology for introducing the outside right, Rogers, in our last home game. This player was introduced to the club as the old Arsenal/Newcastle United/Chester player. Being short of players we were forced to play this man with unfortunate consequences. I have now found out that we were hoodwinked, although his inept display was sure evidence of his inability to play. We will leave it at that.'

Southend United goalkeeper Ted Hankey sneaked away from his Royal Artillery unit to play under an assumed name for the reserves against Reading and lost his sergeant's stripes when his deception was discovered. Liverpool's Billy Liddell had better luck. Posted to an RAF camp at Heaton, near Manchester, he discovered that personnel were not allowed out until 4.30 p.m. on Saturdays. Liverpool were playing Manchester City at Maine Road and when Liddell's application to be released at midday was refused, he climbed over the wall and joined up with his teammates at the railway station. Military police were checking passes outside the station but they ignored the party of footballers and Liddell, who later became a JP, got away with it.

A WOMAN'S WAR

The Second World War, just like the First, for ever changed the lot of women. Prior to 1939, housewifery, shop work or being 'a domestic' were about the only tasks that women were expected to perform. But with the bulk of Britain's manpower serving in the military after 1939, eventually women were also required to do some form of National Service, if not in the services themselves then certainly in the Land Army or in munitions factories. Then it was my mother's turn to panic. She had not worked since her late teens and when, in the spring of 1942, two men 'from the Ministry' turned up on our doorstep attempting to register her for factory work, I can imagine her shock. Eventually, she wriggled out of it by agreeing instead to provide billets for servicemen.

She was in the minority. By the middle of 1943, almost ninety per cent of single women in Britain, and eighty per cent of married women, were working in factories, on the land or in the armed forces.

Factory work could lead to romance in the unlikeliest way. Margaret Naisbett wrote her name on a shell she was packing at the Aycliffe Ordnance Works, County Durham. Gunner Arthur Shepperson loaded the twenty-five-pounder into his artillery piece

and later wrote to Margaret to tell her that it had landed among
Italian troops. Margaret wrote back to Arthur. In July 1945, they
were married at St John's Church, Darlington.

Women were first called up for war work from March 1941, and
at first that meant single women only, between the ages of twenty
and thirty. Their roles were wide-ranging, from driving ambulances
and fire engines, making munitions and even building ships, to
nursing and working on farms. A few delivered aircraft, and a tiny
handful worked with the Resistance behind enemy lines, none of
which tasks I could ever imagine my mother performing. Factory
work would have been too dirty, agricultural labour too demanding.
And she gossiped too much to make a good spy. No, she was
far better suited to the role of landlady to a few members of His
Majesty's forces.

Around 80,000 served in the Women's Land Army, which was
formed in June 1939. It was not an easy life. The girls looked after
animals, ploughed fields, dug up potatoes, harvested cereal crops,
killed rats, and generally ploughed the fields and scattered seeds for
fifty hours a week.

Some 640,000 of my mother's contemporaries even joined the
armed forces, although of course they did not have to. They served
in the Auxiliary Territorial Service (ATS), the Women's Royal
Naval Service (WRNS) and the Women's Auxiliary Air Force
(WAAF).

The ATS was formed in September 1938, initially as a voluntary
organization that had its roots in the First World War's Women's

Auxiliary Army Corps. At first the roles were much the same – cooks and clerks, waitresses and telephonists – but later they included the manning (perhaps not the correct word here) of anti-aircraft guns and operating radar. They were banned from serving on the front line but, when the British army evacuated from Dunkirk in May 1940, women telephonists were among the last to leave. Even our present queen did her bit, training as an ATS lorry driver.

Over 700 members of the ATS were killed during the Second World War, and the WRNS lost over 300 personnel, so despite being banned from the battlefield, women could still pay the ultimate price. Reformed in 1939, the Women's Royal Naval Service initially restricted its personnel to clerical and domestic work, but eventually they also worked on small vessels in harbours (but not in open water) as well as performing similar tasks to their ATS counterparts such as radar plotters, meteorologists, bomb-range markers, cipher officers, and flying unarmed aircraft.

Sometimes, things could get confusing, though. An ATS sergeant glared when she saw one of her unit, Winnie Jenkins, strolling through the middle of Slough, wearing civilian clothing and whistling merrily away. The sergeant resolved to put Jenkins on a 'fizzer' for being out of uniform. But a few minutes later, she saw Corporal Jenkins emerge from a shop, smartly dressed and accompanied by her twin sister, who worked in a local factory. To prevent further confusion, Winnie soon found herself posted to another town.

The Women's Auxiliary Air Service was formed in June 1939, its original function clearly stated: to provide drivers, clerical workers, cooks, waitresses and people to take messages. Like the ATS and the WRNS, its roles were soon extended, in their cases to include working on barrage balloon sites and reconnaissance photograph interpretation. Indeed, many 'WAAFs' found themselves very much in the front line, stationed as they were at RAF aerodromes under the thick of the Battle of Britain. Some 900 members of the WAAF died during the Second World War.

Women have always been particularly good at keeping calm and carrying on, but their patience must have been sorely tested between 1939 and 1945, when they were required to take on unfamiliar roles that were normally filled by men who only ended up resenting them for it. In factories and in the armed services, women found many men hostile to their very presence, and even though that hostility mellowed once it became obvious that women were making a positive contribution, they still had to develop a particular sense of humour if they were to survive. It cannot have been easy.

During the war I worked with Group 2 London Civil Defence. There was a former ATS who had been discharged on account of her pregnancy, who became our housekeeper. After the birth of her daughter, Victoria, she returned to our employ. I thought this rather an odd choice of name and asked her: 'Named after the queen?'

'No,' she replied, 'after the station!'

Leila Mackinlay, London

During the war both my twin sister and myself served in the Women's Timber Corps, a branch of the Land Army. We joined, aged eighteen, and stayed in that service until we were twenty-two. During our annual leave we were allowed a travel warrant to the furthest point of England – any travel beyond that point, to Scotland or Wales, and we had to pay our own way.

My sister and myself, and two other friends all stationed in Hereford, decided to use our travel warrants to go to Carlisle and, from there to hitchhike around Scotland as we couldn't afford digs and fares. At Oban we couldn't find a Toc H or a hostel, and couldn't afford the price of a bed and breakfast, so tried to stow away on a boat for the night. Unfortunately, we got caught and were taken by the quartermaster to the local police station. Since the police couldn't help us find cheap lodgings, we begged to be put in a police cell for the night. Eventually we managed to persuade the police that we preferred to be locked up to spending the night outdoors with no shelter.

By law, before being given a bed for the night, we had to have our particulars recorded – our descriptions such as hair colouring and so on. We were shown to our cell and were literally locked in. We couldn't sleep and, at 4.30 a.m., wanted to get out so much that we began banging on the door and shouting. It took a while, but since we weren't criminals, we were eventually allowed to leave.

A while later, I sent a parcel of Herefordshire apples to the policeman who had taken care of us. He replied, assuring us that the apples were delicious and that we had been 'lovely' prisoners, who were 'a joy to lock up'.

Ann Kent, Sandbach

During the war years I was working with the Land Army. There were a lot of Englishmen, but also Italian prisoners of war. The weather in one particular summer was wet and there was a lot of spreading of lime to be done. These prisoners' English vocabulary was very limited but the local boys were intent on teaching them their swear words.

One particular day, Renado, who always called me 'Siliva', came back while I was milking and called to me: 'Siliva, lime no bloody good, similar shit!' Loosely translated, he meant that the rain had made the lime so sticky that it was comparable with cow manure. Surrounded as I was by other workers, I was so embarrassed.

Sylvia Chaplin, Truro

My sister was a nursing sister in a hospital in Liverpool. One day a woman arrived at the hospital's maternity ward. Upon admission, she was asked for the name of her husband. She told the staff that her husband had been a prisoner of war in Germany for the past two years. When she was asked how she came to be expecting a baby if this was the case, she replied: 'Oh, but he's written, you see!'

Evelyn Whalley, Southport

As a student nurse, I was based on a maternity ward when an unmarried middle-aged lady was admitted to have her baby. She was accompanied by her mother, a traditional type who kept crying and saying: 'It was them there soldiers, they've been manoeuvring around our village again!'

ANONYMOUS, IPSWICH

The best war cartoon of my recollection had to do with the policy of removing UXBs to distant open spaces for defusing. There was the man seated on the upper deck of a bus with a huge bomb on the seat beside him. The conductress approaches and he asks for 'One and a half to Hackney Marshes.'

Leila Mackinlay, London

Working with the Land Army, it was one of my jobs to wash the cows' udders, prior to the attachment of the automatic milkers. One of the other girls was an inveterate telltale, although nobody took much notice of her. I'd just finished my washing one day when the cowman came in.

'She's missed that one!' the triumphant telltale exclaimed.

'She'd have a job with that one,' the cowman replied, 'it's a young bull!'

Miss P. Manser, Maidstone

About 1942, our Scottish GCO decided he would organize a Christmas party. Situated, as we were, at the then North-Western Polytechnic in Kentish Town, we had the correct facilities. It was decided that everyone should try to dress up a bit and the girls all managed some sort of party dress. Inevitably there were Scottish reels and the WVC lady, small but with an ample bust, had on a tight evening skirt and low-necked blouse. I can still see the fascinated eyes of the men, happily anticipating the worst. I hasten to say this never happened, but it looked a near thing.

Leila Mackinlay, London

I was working in the NAAFI and was happy at the barracks I'd first been posted to, but in wartime nobody was a fixture so, when the need arose for my services elsewhere, I had my marching orders. My next posting was at a canteen by a gun site perched on farmland overlooking the town and docks, and here I was nightly tumbled out of bed to the tune of a naval gun booming its anger at German aircraft. This gun shone beautifully when viewed by daylight. But, when darkness fell, it became an angry dragon spitting fire.

The stove on which I had to cook was an antiquated 'iron maiden' which was heated by coal. This monster required a lot of care and attention if it was to serve me well. I had already met one like it. The gunners on KP duties had no idea how to treat this thing. They forgot this baking machine had vents and holes in various places and that, unless these were kept free of soot, my rock cakes would turn out like pancakes . . .

After a few days of using a temperamental oven, I decided to discontinue the services of the KP brigade and clean the stove myself. When I had complained about the stove, the boys always had some excuse. The wind was blowing from the wrong direction, or it was poor-quality coal. I found the flues full of soot. Anyone with such a dirty bottom had a right to misbehave. But after a vigorous brushing from me the oven carried out its work once more.

At the barracks it had not been too noisy, but on the gun site the sound of voices shouting 'Who goes there?' and the gun booming kept us awake at night. As I lay awake I began to worry about the oven and whether it would let us down the next day. One particularly nervous girl predicted we would get murdered in our beds and, by the end of a trying day, I predicted that I should be the one to murder this complaining female!

Gwyneth Wright, London

Besides being at Group 2, I did off-duty driving for the WVS and shall always remember a visit to a hush-hush aircraft place where they drew plans, in the heart of the country. It was a lovely hot day. My job was with an official who was checking whether such a small place was entitled to receive an ENSA show. I shall always remember the rictus of a smile on the face of the poor little soubrette attempting to do the splits on the non-slip factory floor.

Leila Mackinlay, London

It wasn't a happy gun site. The faces I saw over the canteen counter were anything but jovial; I had a feeling they were depressed because they hadn't bagged a Jerry plane. And, in their present mood, might shoot at one of our own aircraft by mistake.

Desperate to get to sun-drenched shores, I filled in an application form. I had little time to myself so had to do this while running between the stove and the table, and I hoped that I had not left any greasy fingermarks on the form. I posted it myself, not trusting anyone else enough to allow them to ruin my chances of a posting to a faraway place. In the meantime, I found myself transferred to a new canteen a few miles away. Although the voice of the guns could still be heard, they could not be felt and this new canteen was a much more pleasant environment. I began to forget about the possibility of endless blue skies and to enjoy the rain and fog of the British climate.

Eventually I received my reply. I had to go to Manchester for another medical and, since I would be under the protection of the army while posted overseas, I would need a few weeks of training.

I arrived in Manchester just as the heavens opened and landed at the YWCA looking like a refugee with water dripping from all directions. My shoes squelched as I walked to the reception desk. Here I spent the night. By morning the warm atmosphere of the building had partially dried my coat, but my shoes still had that musical tone about them.

My stomach churned at the idea of the medical. I do not like doing the stripping act before strangers and I knew before the day was over many MOs' beady eyes would find fault with my chubby torso. I was prodded and poked in many delicate areas. Questioned about my grandparents and parents.

Many more personal questions were asked about me and I wondered if I was to enter the Intelligence Corps, rather than be a baker of buns! The amount of blood taken from me could have caused anaemia, and the urine I had been expected to produce left me feeling empty. The MO who took my blood pressure nearly had me joining the barrage balloons with his pumping. By the end of the day, any modesty I had had been taken away and I felt like a 'fallen woman'.

A large cup of tea soon had my kidneys in working order and my blood pumping once more. I left Manchester to its rain and made my way back to the canteen to wait for the letter that would beckon me towards the training course.

It took the army a few weeks to decide if the enemy was ready to face me and my rock buns, but a letter eventually came inviting me to spend twenty-eight days at a barracks in Wigston near Leicester.

I arrived there with a few more rookies and here a new era in my life began. The day at the quartermaster's stores was a great laugh. I joined the line of girls at the stores and saw a few soldiers standing behind the counter. And behind those soldiers were shelves holding various pieces of ladies' underwear. As I came towards the counter, a large kitbag was thrown in my direction and into this I placed 'three of everything' which was thrown over the counter at me. Each soldier behind the counter must have had a perverted sense of humour because, with one look at each girl, they passed those garments without enquiring the size, and when I dared question the size of one garment coming my way I was told, brusquely: 'You can swap with someone!'

Would I find a Tessie O'Shea to fit the drawers I held in my hand? I managed to get to the end of the line without starting a civil war, whereupon a topcoat was thrown over my head to stop me arguing with the supply corporal, and a cap planted in a drunken manner over that!

As I moved my load I knew there was one thing they had forgotten to issue – a porter to carry this lot to the barrack room.

I struggled back to my room and, with some relief, dropped the bag of tricks upon my bed. As I unpacked, I discovered various sizes of underwear from one that would have fitted Twiggy. So a swapping session began, with screams of delight coming from the girls who managed to find something to fit.

The khaki shade of 'passion killers' would have turned off even the most sex-starved male, but maybe the army had a point there! When I tried to exchange a pair of these khaki bloomers for a smaller size, I was told that they would soon shrink in the wash. I never found out if that were true. I used them as shoe shiners and very good at it they were too.

Gwyneth Wright, London

I worked on the buses during the war and had many a laugh. One day a man climbed aboard with a monkey. We had special 'dog' tickets, but not monkey tickets! So I punched a hole in a dog ticket for the little thing. The monkey snatched it out of my hand as I proffered it to its master and began to chew it. 'Please yourself,' I told the monkey, 'but if the inspector gets on, you'll have to pay again!'

Mrs Z. Price, Withington

Foundation garments were made like chastity belts, and these were placed in the bottom of my kitbag for the duration, along with bras that pulled down rather than uplifted the bust, and a few more khaki 'fashions' saw the light only on inspection day.

The shoes issued almost crippled me for life when I introduced them to my feet. We had been advised to have a size larger than we would normally wear, but I found I had to shuffle my feet to keep them on during marches. I demanded a size smaller, only to find that my feet were soft and the new shoes hard. I squeezed and prodded the leather of those clodhoppers to soften them, but only after several blisters did those shoes and my poor feet become good friends.

I feel sure the girls who, like me, had been attracted by a spirit of adventure, regretted making their application after a few days at the barracks. Each morning in PT kit, looking like a bunch of schoolgirls, we pranced around the parade ground for exercises that the male sergeant insisted was 'making the blood circulate'.

My blood was always at boiling point after being called many unpleasant names if we did anything wrong on parade. With all this arm stretching, I thought mine would leave their sockets, and I discovered many muscles that I had never used before.

When the sergeant told us we were the 'doziest lot he had ever met', we became determined to show him. Muttering our hatred of him, we marched like dedicated soldiers kicking hell out of the tarmac as we gritted our teeth. We were entirely unused to this sort of thing. The only walking I had done lately was between stove and table, and I ached in every bone in my body. All visions of faraway places died, because I felt sure that if I ever left those barracks alive, it would only be as a permanent invalid. Somehow I survived and left the world of marching and exercise, and pressing uniforms and cleaning shows and lectures on VD and how not to become pregnant, a much fitter person with a few pounds off my rump.

I was now a Lieutenant Corporal and I found out later why it was necessary for all that exercise. To give us muscles to carry our kit and strength to ward off all those wrestlers among the soldiers we would meet while earning our 'defence' medal.

Gwyneth Wright, London

Several refugees from the Bath blitz were staying at a Somerset farm near Burnham-on-Sea, where I spent several wartime breaks. It seemed the ladies of Bath had the idea that the wearing of corsets would somehow help protect them against the blasts.

The farmer had three spinster sisters-in-law who had moved in with them for the duration. One day, with the bathroom door half open, he was heard to pray for God to 'give him patience with his lot'.

One of the Bath refugees died while staying there. Petrol restrictions made funerals difficult, especially when the nearest crematorium was not nearby. All that was permitted was one hearse. Mourners were expected to travel by train. The farmer said that if the relatives of the lady wouldn't mind his coming with them – he needn't attend the service if they preferred – the necessary petrol coupons would be available, since he had to be back for milking.

Leila Mackinlay, London

Some of the other bus conductresses used to wait for me to come in, so I could relate some of my experiences. We did have some fun! I once had to appear at Derby Assizes when a lunatic hit me at New Mills. He was what they called a 'moon maniac'. His wife, poor dear, waited for me because she wanted to apologize for him. It appears he had trouble that day with the police and they were looking for him when he attacked me. His wife had just had her eighth child, and was only thirty-four. He went home at dinner time and asked her to go to bed with him. She refused, saying she wasn't fit. So he chased her out of the house with an axe. He gave the police a letter that read: 'I hereby state, that tonight I will murder my wife and eight children.' The envelope was addressed: 'To anyone, anywhere.'

Mrs Z. Price, Withington

During the war, the Venerable Archdeacon of Gibraltar used to stay at the farm with his wife. He had an old-fashioned ear trumpet, which my friend and I found extremely amusing. He felt anxious to help and, as conversing was a bit dicey, he liked to pour out the tea or coffee at breakfast. Alas, he was apt to mix them up somewhat, so we used to rush down to avoid 'Te-offee', as we coined it. He loved painting and, without his ear trumpet, would station himself in the road sketching. Looking over his shoulder at one particular sketch, my friend said: 'But there aren't any apples on that tree!'

A little reproachfully he replied: 'No, I like them there!'

Leila Mackinlay, London

For seven years I was a nurse on an ambulance – and many times during the war I had to be its driver, too. At night I used an American ambulance because I was in with the patient and, if I was alone, I could still drive and keep my eye on them.

Once, after taking a casualty from Hurn Aerodrome to a London hospital, and having done a twenty-four-hour stint, I stopped on the

Hog's Back near Guildford for a short sleep before continuing south to my base. When I awoke, a convoy of Americans was passing, going on to embark at Southampton. I tagged on the end of this convoy and, a few miles further on, they stopped for refreshments. Of course, I stopped too. An orderly came up to me and said: 'I'm bringing your coffee and sandwiches, sister.'

I realized that they thought that, being in an American ambulance, I was part of their convoy. I was desperately hungry and scoffed up the coffee and eats before they realized that I wasn't with them. When they moved off, I again tagged on until we came to the crossroads where the convoy went on to the docks and I turned right for home. I've often wondered since if, once they got to Southampton docks, they thought they'd lost an ambulance.

Irene Stevenson, Christchurch, Dorset

I was serving in the ATS and my greatcoat was much too long, so I decided to shorten it by several inches. After cutting off quite a bit of material, I tried it on to check the length. But when I put my hands in the pockets, I had a shock – the articles therein weren't mine! I'd cut up the coat of the girl in the next bed by mistake. Fortunately, she was my best friend and saw the funny side of it.

B. Cole, Mablethorpe

I was in the ATS during the war and one Christmas was determined to go home. As all travel for us was cancelled, I had civvies sent from home. They included a two-piece suit comprising a skirt and a jacket. The skirt was much too big but, as it was Hobson's Choice, on it went. On the train journey home I was in a compartment with naval personnel and civilians, all of whom were teasing me, saying that surely I must be in the forces, a girl my age, etc. . . . I kept denying it until the train drew into my station, whereupon I jumped up – and down fell my skirt to reveal a pair of khaki knickers! It was with much laughter – and my blushes – that I hurriedly hauled the skirt up again and made my escape.

Joyce McDiarmid, Kirkintilloch

During one stay on the farm I had a young singer friend (later with ENSA) stay with me, and the farmer and his wife, who were keen Methodists, asked whether she might sing for them in chapel. She had to borrow both stockings and hat to make her appearance, where she planned to sing 'Ave Maria' and 'Oh, For The Wings Of A Dove'. Doubting my ability to keep a straight face during her recital, I absented myself. As I stood to one side I heard the poor organ boy almost forget to work the bellows, in his wonderment at this glamorous creature.

Leila Mackinlay, London

An ATS driver was ordered to drive an army VIP from Caterham to Aldershot. There was no time for anything but to get going but, about halfway, she spotted a ladies' lavatory and asked if she could take a very short break. The VIP said: 'Yes, I don't mind waiting a minute.'

While she was gone, the VIP thought that he might as well also take the opportunity and went to the gents. The driver came back, jumped in the car, and sped on to Aldershot. When she arrived, she opened the passenger door – and there was no VIP. She had left her vital cargo marooned outside a gentlemen's lavatory miles away.

Anonymous, relating a story told
to them by an army chaplin

I was in the ATS, stationed at Aldershot. It would be the summer of 1943 or 1944. One dinner time, the orderly officer doing the rounds asked the usual: 'Any complaints?'

Normally, no one dared speak up. But this time, one girl said: 'Yes ma'am, there are dead flies in the chips.'

The officer went into the kitchen and came back a few minutes later. 'I'm sorry,' she told us, 'the flies are falling from the ceiling into the hot fat. Just put them to one side and eat the chips.'

Another danger at mealtimes was to do with the prunes and custard. Recruits passed the warning on to all newcomers: 'If you get a prune with legs on it – it'll be a cockroach!'

Barbara Leach, Skipton, North Yorkshire

I was a WAAF during the war and stationed on a balloon site near Portsmouth. We had a bucket toilet but we had to get two grappling hooks and carry the toilet to a great big well on the site, take the lid off, and empty the toilet into this well. One time we forgot to put the iron lid back on the well. We went to bed in the Nissen hut, leaving two guards on duty. One girl came home quite late, crept away from the guards, then fell into the well. Her screams were awful and woke us all up. If you could have seen the mess of her and the stench. Poor soul! We got seven days' pay stopped for not putting the lid back on and she had seven days' jankers [restriction of privileges] for coming in late!

Our balloon blew away one night when we should have been on guard. You see, every time the wind changed, and the balloon is bedded on the ground, you had to turn the balloon into the wind. We were both having cocoa at the time. When we came out, the balloon had gone. We were panic-stricken. We woke the sergeant and she said: 'You'll have to get a new one up right away!'

So all twelve of us were up working all night long to put up another balloon as an air raid had started. We had a severe reprimand and fourteen days' pay stopped. Didn't we suffer? But we enjoyed it all really!

Mrs J. Evans, Loughton, Essex

I was in the ATS from 1939 until 1944, stationed most of the time with the Royal Army Pay Corps at Bournemouth. One of our number was returning from leave when she had a slight accident. She caused great amusement by sending the following telegram to the CO:

'Unable to return. Fell at Waterloo.'

E. Barrett (née Clampit),
St Leonards-on-Sea

We were in a large ATS barrack room sleeping in double-tier bunks. One morning I put out my hand for my shoes, only to find water, quite a few inches of it too. If that was a shock, imagine how I felt when I saw two ducks placidly swimming towards me. There had been heavy rain and wind during the night, the outside door had blown open, and in came the deluge – and the ducks.

Joyce McDiarmid, Kirkintilloch

At the end of 1939, I joined the WAAFs as a sparking plug tester, but it was decided that WAAFs would take over from men to man barrage balloon sites, which was a very tough and strenuous job and the only branch of the WAAFs where you received equal pay to the men, and the only branch which you could not re-muster into another job.

The balloons had to be unshackled and as the cable was paid out from the winch, the guy ropes had to be held until the balloon was at the point of detachment and the tail guy rope was held to the last, before the balloon was sent up. Well, the girl who was at the engine paying out the cable, must have put her foot on the accelerator because the next thing I knew, I was a few feet from the ground. I was petrified when I looked down. I didn't know whether to hang on or jump! All the girls on the site were shouting out to the girl on the winch to stop the engine and I think she had as much of a fright as me when she saw me up there. I decided that the only thing I could do was to let go of the rope and I landed, twisting one of my feet quite badly. I had to have it strapped up for quite a time and I still have problems with that foot to this day. It wasn't that funny at the time, but when I think how funny I must have looked – a good buxom wench like me, dangling up in the air on the end of that rope – I certainly have a laugh about it now.

Mrs K. P. Ross, Northolt, Middlesex

The scene is a small ward adjoining a general ward of a military hospital. A patient is brought in with a bad cough. He is under guard and is put to bed in a small one-bed ward adjoining the long general ward. The guard makes himself as comfy as possible with a hard chair and a newspaper. Night comes, and with it the change of staff. The night sister is kind and jolly, but also very busy. The orderly is new, but eager to please.

During the small hours coughing is heard from the small room. It persists and at last sister pours out some cough mixture and calls the orderly saying: 'Here, give this to the poor fellow.'

There is silence for a short time, then the coughing starts again. Again, sister calls the orderly and, pouring out a sleeping draught says: 'Give this to the poor man – he must have some rest. I'll be along in a minute.'

When she enters the small room a few moments later, she has a shock. The guard is about to drink the sedative. The patient is sleeping peacefully.

G. A. Jennings, former VAD
attached to the RAMC

The following took place just after lunch on a warm summer's afternoon during 1943 and was reminiscent of a Brian Rix Whitehall farce. For the duration of the war I was employed in the Admiralty within a very important office unit comprising naval officers but also staffed with civilian clerks and typists.

The officer in the incident was a young lieutenant, a bachelor, whose home was in the West Country and who lived in London in a service club. Lacking the services of mum, or other female family member to rally round with the occasional sewing job, he relied upon his secretary to help him out now and then for any minor, but necessary, tailoring tasks.

On this particular afternoon he had the misfortune to acquire a lengthy split along the seam of his trousers in the nether region. He arranged with his secretary to pass the trousers out to her for mending at her desk in the other office. He solved the problem of what to wear in the meantime by draping around his waist a tartan travelling rug that he kept in the office and used for sleeping when duty officer.

The first part of the operation went well, and he returned to his desk where his strange apparel was hidden when he sat down. Unfortunately, the sewing job was delayed by several lengthy telephone calls that his secretary had to deal with. Before she had time to complete the repair, the young lieutenant had a visitor, a high-ranking naval officer from one of the Southern Commands, with many impressive rings of gold braid adorning his sleeves.

The messenger who had conducted the visitor from the main entrance ushered him into the office of the lieutenant, who immediately rose to his feet to greet his superior officer with suitable deference to his rank, completely forgetting his unorthodox garb.

The visitor's bemused look took in the spectacle of the lieutenant standing there in his naval uniform, but clad from the waist downwards in a red tartan sarong, finishing just below his knees and displaying his socks and suspenders.

Just then his secretary, flustered by the delay, rushed in with the trousers, nearly knocking the visitor over and exclaiming: 'We should have done this after the office closed!'

On seeing the visitor, her mouth opened and closed like a goldfish.

Then she dropped the trousers on the floor, and fled before anyone could say anything. Lieutenant X retired, red-faced, to complete his attire while the visitor was pacified with a cup of tea, over which everything was explained.

Mrs D. Faithfull, Pinner, Middlesex

At the beginning of the war, my London office was evacuated to a newly built block of flats in Surrey. All our young boys either volunteered or were called up in their various age groups. Many joined the RAF or the Royal Navy. Some served with distinction and always came to see us when on leave. Naturally, we felt a great pride in 'our' boys. So when in 1942 the older sample were called up, they also came to see us and had the usual spate of questions to answer.

One of those that returned was Henry, who joined the RAF and came to see us in his aircraftsman's uniform a few months later. He had been in our office several years and was a reserved, quietly spoken fellow, not given to much obvious humour. The questioning went like this:

Us: Are you going to be a pilot?
Henry: Oh, no.
Us: What then? A navigator?
Henry: Oh, no.
Us: But you will learn to fly?
Henry: Oh, no.

Us: Why ever not?

Henry: I don't particularly want to.

Us: Then you'll have to be a gunner or something?

Henry: Oh, no. I'll be ground staff.

Us: What? A penguin?

Henry: I think that's what they call them.

Us: But you will serve overseas, and you'll have to fly to get there.

Henry: Oh, I hope not.

Us: Why? Don't you want to serve overseas and help in the fight?

Henry: Oh, no. Not in wartime.

Us: Not in wartime? What do you mean?

Henry: Not in wartime. It's far too dangerous.

There were no more questions. We simply laughed ourselves silly but Henry remained quite serious.

Gwen Harris, Oxted, Surrey

Here are some extracts I saved from letters to
The Pensions Office:

'I am glad to say my husband was reported missing.
He is now dead.'

'I cannot get sick pay. I have six children. Can you tell
me why?'

'This is my eighth child, what are you going to do
about it?'

'In reply to your letter I have already co-habited with
your officers, so far without results.'

'I am writing this for Mrs J. She expects to be
confined next week and can do with it.'

'I am sending my marriage licence and six children I
have. One died, who was baptized on half a sheet of
notepaper by Rev Thomas.'

Betty Quigley, Glasgow

I was a special constable in Scunthorpe during the war. One early morning, during an air raid, a bus drew up alongside me and the driver got out.

'Where's the lambing pen, mate?'

I looked at him in surprise since he seemed to have a bus full of passengers rather than a lorryload of sheep.

'I've thirty-six pregnant women here that I want to get rid of!' I directed him quickly to the nearby maternity home.

G. F. Leawing, Lincoln

Things could get awfully mixed up during the war. My wedding day took place on 5 September 1939, two days after war was declared. My fiancé, Sidney Glasby, and my brother, William, decided to have a double wedding at our local registry office. The registrar was away so a young man took his place. It was his first duty. He nearly married me to my brother, making us stand side by side without bothering to find out who was with whom, until we enlightened him.

Lucy Glasby (née Harris),
Clapham Junction

On another occasion I was working at a housing estate. There were some forty-six incendiary roof fires during one raid and a housewife told me she'd been unable to stir her man, a former trawlerman who'd been serving on minesweepers and was enjoying a bit of leave with a drink or two, to join her in the shelter. I was on watch for incendiary targets and I saw one go right through the roof of her building. I took my stirrup pump and bucket and entered the building and went up to her upstairs flat. I shouted, trying to locate the man, but there was no reply. When I got upstairs I checked each room, one at a time. Eventually I found both the man snoring away, and the hole in the ceiling of the bedroom. Smoke came from a hole in the bed, between the chap's legs. The bed was on fire. He was coughing and snorting, but didn't wake. I got the stirrup pump and started to put out the fire and he began to stir. When he realized his situation he leapt from the bed. He pulled the bed over on its side and we saw that the bomb had gone right through a spiral bedspring into the floor, where it had stuck on a joist. With the fire extinguished he told the chief that he'd been so fast asleep that, if it hadn't been for me, he would have 'lost his lot'. I knew he was stinking drunk, but said nothing. I think it was very easy to get like that for men coming home on leave.

Mrs J. W. Graham, Lanarkshire

It was one of those beautiful evenings that close one of June's perfect days. We three, loathe to go into the house, sat in the garden talking and remembering other nights that we'd shared as drivers in the ARP service.

We were becoming enveloped in a long silence of perhaps sombre memories of those far-off times, when I reminded the others that it was twenty-two years ago exactly since Hitler had begun his doodlebug attacks, sending waves of the first of his secret weapons. They caused such widespread damage that communications were getting very strained, and the ambulance and rescue squads were getting adept at judging just where the fall would be after the V1 engine cut out. Not waiting for official instructions, most of the personnel would be on incidents – destinations unknown – leaving the depot bare of manpower.

About 2.30 a.m., a call for the mobile canteen came in. Like so many of the vehicles used by the ARP, it had been converted from an ambulance to its present use. It was pretty ancient, its gear lever was on the right-hand side and you could see the road through the gears. It had been fitted with a fifty-gallon water tank over the driver's seat, and if you wanted to turn a corner without the vehicle toppling over, you always saw to it that the tank was full. One side of the vehicle had been made to open up, forming a canopy over the counter. Someone had always to be inside to rescue something or other that moved from its moorings.

This night, when the call came, there was only one other person beside the depot chief who could come with me, and that was the cook who had stayed on all night, as she was too frightened to go home. She wasn't a particularly bright person, but was willing to go in the back. I asked her to get a crate of milk loaded, only to be told there were only two quart-bottles until the milkman came. Heavens! Eighteen cups to a pint – that wouldn't go far.

I told her to keep things like the primus stoves on the floor as much as possible, and that when I banged twice she should start filling some cups before pulling up the flap, and so be ready for the big rush when it came.

The sky was just beginning to get that pearly look of the dawn, but there was still the throbbing of German bombers and the sound of distant gunfire. It was a terrible business remembering to use your right hand to change gear, and I always had to look down. So I was unable to stop a friendly warden when he banged twice on the side of the van in greeting.

From the back of the van there was a terrific rending sound and a bang. Stopping, and hopping out round to the back, I saw that, at what the cook thought was my signal, the flap had been opened and sheared off as I'd passed a lamp post before pulling up. Poor cook was looking a bit white and strained, but I said not to worry and placed the flap against the wall so that we could collect it on the return journey. She'd placed all the cups and saucers out on the counter too, and they were a bit of a shambles.

A short way down the road, I began to pull into a clear space when, without warning, the road caved in and the front wheels sank down to rest on a pipe of some sort. The noise from the back was ominous. I had visions of scalding water, the floor awash with tea, and a prostrate cook. I tentatively opened the door and wanted to laugh, and yet could not, at the sight of all that broken crockery, the urns slowly dribbling out tea into the sink, and the cook, who had come to rest sitting in a bucket, clasping the two quart-bottles of milk. Out of the debris we salvaged a dozen or so cups, and for anyone very thirsty, a few saucers. It all became a bit hilarious, with hands snatching cups before they'd been rinsed and the queue for saucers, all moaning, while we were trying to get used to standing at an angle.

On returning to the depot and leaving the canteen to be towed out, we found another job lined up. A young baby, just three days old, had been injured and was in hospital. Its mum was unharmed in the rest centre, and every three hours we would be collecting her to feed her baby. It was 5 a.m. The milk round had started.

May Simpson, Romford, Essex

Another time, a bomb hit a hose that was being used to fight a fire caused by incendiaries and all the water cascaded all over us. We were wet through – but cheerful.

For two weeks we were evacuated from Woolwich Hospital down to Farnborough. One night there was a noise on the roof and this turned out to be a German airman who had baled out of his bomber. I don't suppose he thought that was funny, but we did.

Betty Sheperdson, York

I was a full-time Civil Defence volunteer and my husband, who had an artificial limb and was employed on the Tyne by a well-known shipbuilding and engineering firm, was a part-time CD volunteer. We were always busy as there were many 'guest nights', as we called the air raids, most of which seemed to come on moonlit Friday nights.

During one particularly heavy raid, with ack-ack fire going on and shrapnel crashing down, my husband was manning his post when he heard two seamen coming up the main road, pretty drunk and singing and staggering about. He yelled: 'Come on you fellows, take cover,' and then went back to his post. When I got down there I discovered two very wet chaps. There was a brick-built public shelter nearby, but in their inebriated state they had mistakenly stumbled into a demonstration Anderson shelter that was awaiting removal. It had filled with water and the pair were drenched. They spent the rest of the night in the public shelter, soaked to the skin from the waist down, but very sober. My husband made them hot coffee and I took this to them along with a couple of blankets to warm them up. They were particularly unhappy because, somewhere along the way, they had lost the bottles from which they had been drinking. The following day, when the Anderson shelter was pumped out, lying in it were two bottles of Newcastle Brown Ale and half a bottle of rum.

Another night I discovered two bearded sailors hunkered down against the wall, talking to my husband. They said they'd have preferred to take their chances at sea because they felt safer aboard a moving target.

Mrs J. W. Graham, Lanarkshire

One early summer's day, after I'd been through a high concentration of tear gas while training in full uniform but minus respirator, I travelled home on a bus. I sat close to the open entrance because of the effect the tear gas had on my eyes. However, as the bus filled – eventually there were people standing – I caught sight of some passengers surreptitiously wiping their eyes and blowing their noses. When I rang the bell to get off, the conductress, a friend of mine, was upstairs taking fares. When she came down, she said: 'I could understand this lot with hankies at the ready in winter, but what's the matter with them today I don't know.' You can guess that I did, but I didn't dare say a word. My uniform had become impregnated with the tear gas, and as the vehicle filled and heated, the gas started to react until the whole of the lower-deck passengers were getting very weepy-eyed. They just didn't know why.

Mrs J. W. Graham, Lanarkshire

I was a nurse on nights at the Woolwich Hospital when at 5 a.m. on 14 September 1940, a high-explosive bomb hit the big main wards. I was buried under the rubble and I still think it was a miracle that I survived unharmed, except for cuts and bruises. I wormed my way up and out and carried on helping to move the patients. Then it was noticed that I had a great red stain on my back, but investigations proved it to be from a bottle of ink. Matron kept asking me: 'Where is your cap, nurse?' My hair was piled high with debris, dust etc. and I was also stone deaf for about two hours and she was worried about my cap. Years later, when excavations began, my cap-brim was found under all the rubble, but the rest of the cap was lost for ever.

During one air raid, all our electric lights failed just as a baby was about to be born. However, we did have a gaslight that was quickly put to use and the baby was safely delivered. Then a bomb hit St Mary's Churchyard at Woolwich, and we were told that the coffins flew about in all directions. One corpse had the chin still strapped up.

Betty Sheperdson, York

THROUGH
CHILDREN'S
EYES

Time changes everything. When, in 1978, I first made an
appeal for amusing stories from the Second World War,
many of those who responded were middle-aged men and
women. They had seen the war through the eyes of a child. Their
perception of life on the Home Front was entirely different to those
who were already adults when war was declared.

One such man was Jim Phelps, in 1978 a forty-eight-year-old
recreation officer with Derby City Council. On 3 September 1939,
Jim was nine years old and one memory of that Sunday morning had
remained with him. Tears streaming down the faces of his neighbours
finally brought home to young Jim the reality of it all. Up until then,
war had been a game played with lead soldiers and a toy cannon
that fired matchsticks. But on the morning of Sunday 3 September
1939, Jim saw his mother's friends hugging and weeping. For the
second time in a generation, Britain had declared war on Germany.
In that moment he did a lot of growing up.

'I went to bed on the Saturday, wondering what the morning would bring. At 11.15 a.m., we tuned in our wireless and heard the prime minister, Neville Chamberlain, announce that we were at war. I was so excited, I ran into the street to find my pals. Then I saw some of the neighbours. They could remember the last war. They were weeping. Suddenly I realized what it meant.'

Jim spent the remainder of the day helping to fill sandbags around his neighbourhood. At 3.30 a.m., the air-raid sirens sounded for Derby's first alert of the war. The Phelps family trooped to the public shelter nearby. Nothing happened. It was a false alarm. Of course, the sirens wailed many more times and sometimes they did herald German bombers. To Jim and his pals, though, they generally signalled another adventure. Children are so resilient. They go where adults sometimes fear to tread.

However, like those of adults, children's views of the war depended a great deal on where they lived. Jim's hometown suffered air raids but remarkably little death or destruction by comparison to bigger cities, from where children were evacuated to smaller towns and to the countryside. In the first few weeks of the war, almost two million children were moved from cities that the government feared would become primary targets for German air raids. The scheme was voluntary and its take-up varied wildly from city to city. While seventy-five per cent of Manchester's children were evacuated, Sheffield gave up only fifteen per cent of its youngsters.

But from wherever they came, and however many, the official account was that it had all gone smoothly and that everyone was happy. In reality, many mothers were loath to wave off their children into the unknown. And when nothing much happened in the first winter of the war – the so-called Phoney War – then thousands of children were taken back to the cities they had left.

Many were glad to be back. The shock of moving from poor

urban housing to villages and farms proved almost impossible to overcome. Their hosts, meanwhile, complained of swearing, bed-wetting, fleas and an increase in local crime. There were also problems where under-fives were accompanied by their mothers who sometimes proved even more troublesome than their offspring. It was a case of two cultures colliding head-on. As a contributor to the Mass Observation Archive put it: 'One half of Britain is now finding out how the other half lives.'

Yet, evacuees or locals, children proved particularly good at keeping calm and carrying on. In 1939, the *Northampton Independent* related the story of a tiny evacuee who greeted his new 'mother' with the words: 'I've just seen a cah!' When she said that she wasn't surprised because there were lots of them about, he replied: 'I know, 'ole 'erds of 'em.'

But children grew up in this war. In December 1945, Jim Phelps, the nine-year-old boy we met earlier, was now sixteen. On Christmas morning he went to his local Methodist Church where there were some German prisoners of war in the congregation. They sat shoulder to shoulder with their fellow worshippers, some of the ordinary people of the town, and together they sang 'Silent Night'.

Jim said: 'My mind went back to that September day when war was declared and I thought about all the horror, the hurt and heartache. And then I wondered what we had learned, and what tomorrow would bring.'

I was given a brand-new football for my twelfth birthday, so I went out in the street to try it out — and kicked it straight through our living-room window. The ball was immediately confiscated. That night, the Luftwaffe carried out a big raid on Southampton. One of the bombs dropped on the road just a few yards from our house, and blew out the rest of our windows. In the morning, I got my football back.

John Summers, Southampton

My father had just bought me a pair of stilts. Being only twelve years old then, I was eager to go out in the street and try them out. Then came the sound of the sirens. I didn't take much notice of it because I'd heard it so many times before. I was up on my stilts in the middle of the road, when all of a sudden I heard a whistling sound. I left my stilts standing and dived for the nearest shop doorway. There was an almighty bang when the bomb hit one of the houses in the nearby street. When it was all clear, I went back to my stilts where they were, still standing in the middle of the road.

Mr R. Durey, Maidstone

I was eight years old when the war started. We lived on the edge of Epping Forest, about eleven miles from Marble Arch. 'Old Wayo' was a man of about sixty-five who loved to get drunk, when he'd the money. He used to come down the road, rolling all over the place, and at the height of an air raid he would shout out to all he could see: 'Jesus'll bomb 'em! Jesus'll bomb 'em!'

By 1944, most people had resigned themselves to a common philosophy: if we are going to die, we may as well die in our beds. So the Anderson shelters were becoming redundant and abandoned. This was just the right atmosphere for a gang of us boys, mostly playing truant from school, to gather and have our fun and games. An old wind-up gramophone was acquired from somewhere and we'd a battered old record that we played night after night. It went: 'Look at the orchids blooming, blooming great flowers, ain't it grand to be blooming well dead?' You can imagine, after a time, the word 'blooming' was substituted by something not so polite.

Towards the end of 1944, the doodlebugs began their blitz on London. One day we were enjoying a swim in the River Roding, boys and girls together, all in the nude – the so-called pre-permissive days – when someone shouted: 'Look up! It's coming straight for us!'

We all jumped out of the water, grabbed what clobber we could and made for one of the trenches that they had dug in the fields to stop Jerry from landing. We had about 400 yards to run and, in our panic, it seemed to follow us. We all sat shivering in the trench, waiting for it to cut out. Luckily, when it did, it crashed in Epping Forest.

In the later war years, an old man by the name of Taters Green, who lodged in a house near me, asked his landlady to get him a bar of soap when she went shopping. When she asked him for his coupons, he replied: 'What? Have they rationed soap as well?'

L. J. Goodey, Loughton, Essex

> Evacuee on being asked to bathe for the second time in two nights: 'Blimey miss, what do you want? An evacuee or a bleeding duck?'
>
> LEILA MACKINLAY, LONDON

Leaving my grandmother's house, my mother and I passed a horse in a field. I said to my mother: 'What's he got a gas mask on under his belly for?' How was a wee girl to know that when a gentleman horse espies a lady horse in the field he becomes aroused? To me, he was wearing a gas mask! My mother bravely managed not to laugh and gave me a suitable explanation.

Brenda Shaw, Kingston upon Hull

Early 1941. It's about 7 p.m. and my mother, father and me, aged eleven years old, are going down to the Anderson shelter in the garden for the night, complete with supper. We're duly settled in, with an oil lamp burning nicely, supper about to be served – crayfish sandwiches for my mother and father; I had a passion for breakfast-sausage sandwiches at that time – when we hear a lone bomber buzzing about, and a frenzied shout of 'Put that light out!' coming from an adjoining road, directed at a near neighbour whose bathroom light is showing brightly. Suddenly, there is the sound of a bomb coming down. Father throws himself over my mother, and she shields me with her body. There's the most terrifying crash as the bomb hits a lamp post and bursts in mid-air, one hundred yards away. The oil lamp is blown out by the blast. I'm crying my eyes out with sheer terror; my father is worried that I've been hit or something. Sheer panic. Then my father says that he has been hit, blood is pouring down his leg. We get the oil lamp lit, Father discovers that the 'blood' pouring down his leg is vinegar for the crayfish sandwiches, and I am howling because I have lost my beloved breakfast- sausage sandwiches. Having sorted out the chaos, we all have a good laugh. Although the laughter is short-lived when we see the damage to our house. But I can still see the funny side of that incident – one among many – after all these years.

Wendy Holliman, Oxhey, Watford

As a boy I lived in Brecon. One of the 'county set' became a special policewoman, and one night mistook the colour of the air-raid warning system. She sounded the siren and all over town, doctors, nurses and firemen crawled out of bed to await the onslaught. Ten minutes later she realized her error and sounded the all-clear. Alas, it was too late to save her brief career.

Revd David Dickery, Newport

When I was a young lad and living in Thesiger Street, Cathays, Cardiff, there used to be a rather rough and ready family called the Hiats. Mr Hiat was a chimney sweep (among other things) and most of the soot he collected would be dumped into the air-raid shelter at the bottom of his garden or, as we used to say, 'out the back'. Like many families, they used to stay under the stairs during the raids.

But this particular night, when Cardiff was really going through it with bombs dropping all over the place, they had no alternative but to dash 'out the back' into the air-raid shelter which was below ground. You can imagine the state of that family, which was a large one, when they emerged next morning covered in soot.

My mother often tells me about the time she took me to the local cinema, The Coronet (the 'Bug-House' we used to call it), when during the performance, the air-raid warning started up. When she got outside the cinema she found that she'd grabbed hold of someone else's little boy, which is quite understandable in the dark and confusion that took place. Not funny for her at the time, of course.

Brian Lee, Cardiff

One other incident comes to mind. I was sitting by the side of a lake at Rickmansworth, enjoying a peaceful afternoon, when I spotted an aircraft in the distance, and commented to my mother that the plane looked as though it was on fire! She lazily looked up from her book, realized it was a doodlebug, grabbed my hand, and we ran along the lakeside to the tent where we were camping. The doodlebug dropped in Mill End, Rickmansworth, and the tent sides 'whoofed' in and out with the blast. My mother suddenly started laughing and I couldn't understand why until she finally stopped, and said: 'How stupid, as if sheltering in a tent would give us any protection if the thing had dropped any nearer!'

Wendy Holliman, Oxhey, Watford

My first day at school took place during wartime. I didn't like school much that first morning, so decided to leave and not go back. I asked some 'big ladies' (I found out later they were sixth-formers playing netball) where the gate was and ran home. Of course, my mother was doing a part-time job and didn't expect me to be back home so the door was locked. She eventually found me sitting in our neighbour's garden eating some chocolate with which the neighbour had pacified me. Needless to say, I got skelped and sent back to school the next day. The teacher was worried, my mother was worried. 'There could have been an air raid.' I was 'a wilful girl' according to the teacher. From that first day I hated school and was never happier than on my leaving day and first job at sixteen. Goodness knows how I passed my 11-plus.

Brenda Shaw, Kingston upon Hull

My late husband was on fire-watching duty one night when he heard an aircraft. As the young boy from next door, who was standing beside him, seemed very worried by this, my husband told him: 'It's all right, son, it's one of ours.' With that the boy ran inside to his family, shouting: 'It's all right, Mam, it's one of Mr Ellis's!'

Mrs F. Ellis, West Bromwich

When the war broke out, all schoolchildren had to be evacuated. Two of mine were sent to Leicester and two to Worthing. When the bombs stopped for a bit over London, the children were brought back home, only to find that very soon the doodlebugs started. So now it was all women and children to be evacuated. We all met at the local school to have tags put on our children. The next day we were taken to the station and off we all went. Nobody knew where we were headed until, after travelling nearly all day, and asking each other where we thought we were going, one little boy shouted: 'I know where we're going, I've just seen a Kentucky Minstrel!'

Well, it gave us mums a good laugh as we realized it was actually a coal miner. We were headed for the Rhondda Valley in South Wales.

Mrs E. Pearce, Woking, Surrey

We had some evacuee children from London in our village. They'd never seen the countryside before. They had no idea where vegetables came from. A friend of mine who took in a brother and sister told me that the children thought that potatoes grew on trees. It was the same with meat and eggs and milk. I don't think they'd ever seen a real-live cow or a chicken, or a pig. But the funniest thing was a small boy who was fascinated by a goldfinch singing away in a tree. He said: 'Look, it's upset. It wants to get back in its cage.'

Beryl Pooley, Kent

My main memory of wartime was bath night. My mother had to bring in the tin bath – I think it was actually made of galvanized iron – from the backyard where it was hung on a nail on the fence. Then it was filled with bucket after bucket of water that had been heated up in the copper. There were five of us kids, and me – being the smallest and youngest – went in last. So you can imagine the state of the water, not to mention that it was only lukewarm by then. But the thing that really sticks in my mind is that the government had said that no one should have more than five inches of water in their bath, to conserve both water and heating. Well, my eldest brother complained about this, saying that since five of us were being bathed in the same water, then we were entitled to twenty-five inches. Then my father pointed out that it was extremely unlikely that an official would come snooping round demanding to see our bath night, anyway. But my mother, bless her, stuck to her guns. 'No,' she said, 'if Mr Churchill says that it's only five inches, then five inches it will be.' And that was that until the end of the war.

Brian Hall, London

Like the adults, us kids were all issued with gas masks. We used to play around in them and I had mine for years after the war. There was one daft little lad in our street – when I say daft, it's just that he was always up to mischief, always on some adventure or other – who went missing one teatime. When he finally turned up at home – he lived a couple of doors away from us – and his mother asked him where on earth he'd been as she'd been worried, he just shrugged his shoulders and said: 'Sitting in the pig-bin, seeing if me gas mask works.'

Roy Marsh, Birmingham

I was twelve when war broke out. At the time my grandmother lived with us and she was a real cantankerous old lady. There was hell to pay when she was told that she had to go and collect her gas mask. She said to me: 'What's the point? Go and have a word with your mother. If we have to go to the shelter, there's no gas laid on there anyway.'

Eileen Jones, Plymouth

Being a young boy during the war, I loved the blackout. I think we all did. We played a game called 'wall-hopping'. The trick was to start at one end of the street, sneak down the passageway into the first garden and get to the other end by climbing over the garden walls. We played soldiers while we were doing it, even blacked up our faces like commandos using burnt cork. Anyway, there was this one neighbour called Mr Bottomer who was a real old grump. He caught me and another lad in his garden and we had the full interrogation. My pal said: 'We just like playing in the blackout. It's more exciting.' And Mr Bottomer said, real angry like: 'Blackout! Bloody blackout! I don't know why they can't fight this bloody war in daylight!'

Maurice Jones, Birmingham

It was a midsummer's early evening – brilliant blue sky, still – and I remember looking up and seeing aircraft high in the sky. We had a lot of what we called 'silverfish' – little insects that used to crawl out of our hearth – and they reminded me of them. Silverfish, high in the blue sky. Then someone said that they were German and all hell broke loose. The man next door had a rifle – I don't know where from but I think he'd served in the First World War – and he was always bragging that it had 'one up the spout', ready for the invasion. So he went to fetch it. Well, by the time he'd returned, the aircraft had disappeared. It was probably relief – relief that we hadn't been bombed, but more relief that the old man hadn't fired his ancient-looking rifle – but everyone in the street fell about laughing. All except the old man, that is. He stormed off back into his house, shouting: 'If that's your attitude, you can fight your own bloody war!'

Ray Smith, Birmingham

One of our neighbours plonked herself down in our house while the bomb-disposal men were dealing with a UXB right outside. She said to my brother: 'Go easy on that jam. There's a war on!' It was hard to ignore with an unexploded bomb in the street outside.

Once, in Victoria Street in London, I saw two ducks happily swimming around an emergency water tank in a bombed-out building. They'd flown in from St James's Park.

June Buckle, London

I was seven years old at the outbreak of war, living in Rochester, near Rochester Airport that was being used by the RAF as a flying training school. We were directly in line for dogfights, stray bombs and anything else that the Germans wanted to drop on us. One afternoon the siren went and we fled to the shelter, accompanied by a neighbour who was on her own. We shut the door just as the sound of the approaching bombers grew louder. Next minute there was a tremendous explosion and the door was blown off. A rush of hot air seemed to come in and we were all hurled into a heap at the back of the shelter. When we eventually recovered, all very shaken, we crawled outside to have a look. A bomb had fallen in the middle of the road and the blast had blown in the front windows, doors etc. The curtains had been torn to shreds and most of the furniture ruined by the flying glass. My mother and neighbour stood speechless, obviously upset. A house four doors up was in ruins, and another bomb had fallen further up the road. The first person on the scene arrived, the local ARP warden, who told my mother off for not being still in the shelter as the all-clear hadn't gone. In no time at all, the street was full of council workers and officials. There was no gas or water – they'd turned it off. My mother and neighbour whose house had suffered a similar fate were upset, naturally, and when a large van of WVS ladies arrived and began brandishing kettles and teapots, my mother asked if we could have a cup of tea. 'It's not for you,' came the reply, 'we have to serve the men filling in the hole first.' And not a cup of tea did we get until every man had been served. Talk about helping the needy . . .

Margaret Pack, Maidstone

I always think I was lucky because during the war we lived in Kent, right under the Battle of Britain. That might sound strange if it came from an adult, but we were just kids. I suppose we spent more time searching around bomb sites, and places where aircraft had crashed, than anywhere else. In the long summer holidays it was great fun. We used to collect shrapnel and anything else we could find and swap it for other things like sweets – which were obviously in short supply – or perhaps even a football, if you had enough 'currency'. Because that is what all these spoils of war were – currency. Sometimes, you'd just swap what you had for a 'better' bit of shrapnel to build up your collection.

Anyway, one day my brother was setting off for work and I was still in bed, and he called up to me that a German plane had been damaged that night and that part of its engine was lying in our front garden. I'd never moved so fast. I got dressed as quickly as I could and raced downstairs. There was no sign of anything in our garden. He was pulling my leg. That was the thing, though – we lived right in the thick of it and we just made a joke of it all. It was just part of our lives.

Len Johnson, London

We were sitting in the air-raid shelter one night. The sirens had sounded but there was no sign of the bombers yet. My parents were discussing the chap down the road who had a bit of a reputation with the ladies. I was only about nine years old and wasn't involved in the conversation but children pick up on these things. Anyway, they were pulling him to pieces when my elder brother – he'd be about fifteen at the time – piped up and said: 'I know why he only goes out with blondes.'

Both my parents stopped talking and just stared at him. Then he said: 'It's because he's afraid of the blackout.' My parents didn't know whether to laugh or tell him off. He told me later that he'd heard the comedian Max Miller crack the joke on the wireless.

Norman Taylor, Lambeth

When I was fourteen, I was evacuated to Hayward's Heath in Sussex. There was a woman and her two-year-old baby living in the same house. Every night she told the little one: 'If you go to sleep, then I'll bring you a nice air raid.' It was the other way round. As soon as the sirens sounded, the baby always dropped off sound asleep.

Eventually I went to work in a factory where they had gas-mask drill. Over the loudspeaker came the order: 'Gas masks on!' and then we had to carry on working until the order came to remove them. Imagine the discomfort. But we just had to carry on.

June Buckle, London

I used to live in a small village where very little ever happened, apart from a few stray bombs that had been targeted at nearby Bomber Command. My father was the local chief air-raid warden and, when the sirens sounded, the wardens gathered at our house.

When my cousin and I were about thirteen, a mock 'invasion' was planned and local people were asked to play the parts of casualties. We were very excited to be able to take part. My cousin had a card pinned to her that read 'Broken leg', while mine read 'Bleeding badly'. We were told to sit under the hedge until the Red Cross found us as we were playing the part of badly injured casualties. We waited and waited and sat and sat. At first we could hear quite a lot of activity, but eventually, as dusk arrived and it fell quiet, we limped out from our hedge to take a look around. There wasn't a soul in sight! We went to the Red Cross hut but it was locked. The exercise had finished, everyone had gone home and we had been forgotten! Desperately disappointed, we went back home to make the cocoa for the boys in the AFS hut. They laughed and laughed.

Mrs M. J. Robertson, High Wycombe

After one heavy raid a block of flats was damaged and sticking out of the rubble was the remains of a grand piano. No wood – just the insides. One of the local kids asked the demolition men: 'If you don't want that old harp, can we have it?'

After another raid, there was this old lady wandering around the street, shouting: 'Sugar! Sugar!' Mum thought she had lost her sugar ration so she sent me out with two spoonfuls. Then she discovered that the old lady was looking for her dog.

June Buckle, London

> Boys will be boys – especially in wartime. At the height of the invasion scare in September 1940, Home Guards reporting for duty in Stockport found that their headquarters had been broken into and seventy-seven rounds of ammunition, some money and a bayonet had been stolen; they assumed it was the work of fifth columnists. But the offenders were much closer to home. Three boys, aged twelve, eleven and nine, appeared before Stockport Juvenile Court, charged with the offence. Two of the boys were sent to a remand home, the third was discharged. And the Home Guard took extra care when securing their HQ for the night.
>
> JOHN ELLIS, MANCHESTER

There was this story that snoek was actually whale meat, although we found out that it was just another sort of fish that came from foreign waters. Anyway, me and my pal, who was a couple of years older than me, were sent to the fishmonger to get some snoek, and my pal asked the fishmonger if it was true – that it really was a whale. And when the fishmonger said that, yes, it was, my mate said: 'Well, in that case, my mum says can you leave the head on for our cat?' The whole shop erupted in laughter.

Derek Taylor, Birmingham

Anyway, we moved to the outskirts of Maidstone but that didn't stop us being bombed. One afternoon the siren went and my mother collected my brother and we crawled under the bed and lay there listening to bombs being dropped on the town about two miles away. Suddenly there was silence. You could have heard a pin drop. Our front door had been left open – it was supposed that a bomb blast would merely rush through the house and out of the back door – and we heard heavy footsteps approaching. 'My God,' whispered my mother, clutching us to her, 'it might be a German!'

We clung to each other as the footsteps came into the hallway and hesitated at the door of the bedroom. 'Anyone about?' said a gruff voice. We breathed a sigh of relief. It was the road sweeper, a man too old to be called up. He stood looking at us as we peered out from the side of the bed and then, without a word, he crawled under my single bed. We all lay there in a long row, saying nothing until the all-clear sounded, whereupon he wriggled out, nodded to my mother and returned to his work.

Margaret Pack, Maidstone

On the way home from school we used to go down Gas Works Lane and watch the gunner over the rail line have a go at any enemy aircraft attacking the trains.

One afternoon it was really going on, guns firing, German aircraft swooping past. Suddenly a huge bang! A bomb had landed, but it bounced up across town and went off in a sports field on the other side. There were tracer bullets everywhere. That was a great afternoon.

One of the neighbours told my mum that she had seen us boys cheering and shouting down by the railway, so she gave me a clip round the ear for not getting home while a raid was going on. Worth it, though.

Ron Finch, Ashford

My father had a big shed in the garden and it was converted into an air-raid shelter. But after the first nights of the Blitz, my mother decided that she would rather die in a warm bed than a cold shed, so she never used it again and, after a while, we all abandoned it in favour of our beds. But it was put to very good use as a 'den' when my two brothers and me, and some of the neighbourhood kids, played together.

To a load of boys with vivid imaginations it was everything – the cockpit of a Lancaster bomber, a submarine under the Atlantic, you name it. We still had to take our gas masks with us, though, and one evening my older brother discovered that if you put your mask on and blew hard enough, then it made a very rude noise. That kept us entertained until bedtime.

Derek Smith, London

I can remember the last day of peace. It was a Saturday and my father took me to see Arsenal play Sunderland. The kick-off was delayed for about two hours because so many children were being evacuated from London that there was traffic congestion everywhere. Arsenal won 5-2 and Ted Drake scored four of them, but everyone was really quiet on the bus going home. I suppose the adults knew that there was going to be a war and that the result of a football match wasn't all that important, considering.

Then one chap said, almost thinking aloud: 'I reckon the Government will declare war on Hitler tomorrow.'

And, quick as a flash, a chap sitting behind him said: 'They can do what they like as long as they don't drag the rest of us in.'

Everyone laughed and it lightened the mood. I was still annoyed, though, when they abandoned the football season and Arsenal's win never counted.

Harry Patrick, London